Web Works

A NORTON POCKET GUIDE

Web Works

Martin Irvine

GEORGETOWN UNIVERSITY

W. W. NORTON & COMPANY

New York • London

Printed in the United States of America
First Edition

The text of this book is composed in Stone Serif
with the display set in Rockwell Bold
Composition by University Graphics, Inc.
Manufacturing by Quebecorp
Book design by Joan Greenfield
Cover design: Suka & Friends Design, Inc., NY

Library of Congress Cataloging-in-Publication Data

Irvine, Martin (Martin J.)
Web Works : Norton pocket guide / Martin Irvine.
p. cm.
Includes bibliographical references and index.
ISBN 0-393-97109-0 (pbk.).—ISBN 0-393-31520-7 (pbk.)
1. World Wide Web (Information retrieval system) 2. Internet (Computer network) I. Title.
TK5015.888.I78 1996
004.6'7—dc20 96-20960

W. W. Norton & Company, Inc., 500 Fifth Avenue, New York, N.Y. 10110
http://www.wwnorton.com

W. W. Norton & Company Ltd, 10 Coptic Street, London WC1A 1PU

1 2 3 4 5 6 7 8 9 0

Contents

Preface

This is not yet another book for "dummies." In fact, *Web Works* is a book for smart people who want to learn the basics for using the World Wide Web and Internet, but who don't want to plow through one of those huge encyclopedias about the Net and Web now available on every bookstore shelf. This is a book for people who want straight answers from the user's point of view. It's a book to keep beside your mouse pad and in a pocket of your laptop case.

Web Works is for students, teachers, businesspeople, people in government and information-intensive professions like law and journalism, and home computer users. My primary aim will be to make the Web understandable and accessible for people who work in schools and universities, businesses, and government. The goal of this book is to provide the right amount of information in an accessible format for beginning and intermediate users of the Net and Web.

Web Works takes the perspective that the Web is the whole of Internet resources. Why? Because the Web as a system embraces or includes earlier Internet technology and ways of moving bits around the Net, and because Web interface software like *Netscape Navigator* is now designed to be a complete front-end to the Net. Learning to use the Web means having access both to what is Web-specific (materials presented in hypertext and hypermedia format) and to all previous and existing Internet resources. Learning the Web means gaining access to the whole Internet.

Web Works and the Web User

It's hard to pick up a magazine or watch the news and not find references to the Internet and the World Wide Web. Every major corporation and information service now commonly advertises addresses for Web pages (their URLs, in Webspeak). Many newspapers and magazines are available on the Web in multimedia versions that have no print equivalent. A Website URL has replaced fax numbers and even email addresses as priority information on business cards. Not knowing how to use the Web places you out of the info-loop. *Web Works* will be your guide to gaining access to this new information resource and to understanding how it works.

Since the Web depends on user-interaction and not passive consumption like other media, we need to know something about how things work and about the key concepts that drive the technology. *Web Works* introduces the Web conceptually from the user's point of view. The great thing about learning the Web and Net conceptually is that we can take what we learn to new contexts: the basics needed by Web users can be readily applied to using any computer running any software for accessing the Web. Learning the key concepts that drive the technology is also important for adapting to the pace of change: specific information for one software package or computer type will quickly go out of date, but conceptual background can always be reapplied. With a few basics under your digital belt, you'll be able to use any Web software package and navigate the Web with confidence and ease.

Learning to use the Web well really means becoming a networked information resources manager. Web navigators soon learn how to make their own connections among kinds of information, synthesizing what's useful for some user-defined end, and ignoring the rest. Other books about the Net and Web have various emphases: *Web Works* assumes that you want to learn how to gain access to usable information and how to make the Web work for you.

Web Works will also be your guide to finding more information about the Web on the Web. *Web Works* is based on an active learning process—you learn the Web by using it. You'll also learn how to do research and make the best use of the searching tools on the Web for finding exactly what you need.

Whenever possible, I will cite sources of information on the Web, rather than print sources. Most of the information you'll need for understanding how the Web works is found on the Web. This makes the Web the world's first intentionally constructed metamedium; that is, since its beginnings, the people involved in the technical development of the Internet and World Wide Web have documented how it works and how to use it. Now there are whole Websites devoted to the Web itself—using it, finding information, and creating your own Web materials.

Using *Web Works*

Since the goal of this book is to introduce readers to how the Web works, I recommend that all readers become familiar with the background in Chapters 1 and 2. These chapters provide an introduction to the key concepts and features of the Net and Web from the user's point of view. For an overview of key terms and concepts, refer to the Glossary on pages 131–44.

If you are using the Web from an office or university LAN, you can skip over Chapter 3, "Getting Connected." If you want the necessary background on getting an Internet connection at home or via an individual phone line anywhere, Chapter 3 then becomes required reading.

Chapters 4 and 5 are the heart of the book for people wanting to use the Web for research or finding needed information efficiently. These chapters will guide you through the best strategies for managing and using information on the Web.

Chapter 6 will introduce other forms of interactive communications that are technically "off the Web" but accessible in an interface to the Internet that can work in concert with Web software.

Chapter 7 builds on the earlier chapters by introducing the expanding hypermedia capabilities of the Web and the kinds of software that users need to know about to use developing and emerging applications of Web media.

With the background of Chapters 1 through 7 and some experience using the Web, you may be interested to learn how to develop your own resources for the Web. Chapter 8 is thus an introduction, and only an introduction, to taking the next step and becoming a Web developer.

And since we're all still undergoing the social and cultural effects of this new networked, multimedia communications environment, Chapter 9 is an attempt to raise some questions and provoke thought about the Web and Net culture.

There is a complete glossary at the end of the book; all technical terms used in the book, and many others that you may encounter as a Web user, are covered there.

The Website for *Web Works*: http://www.wwnorton.com/webworks/

To help you on your way to becoming a skilled navigator and infomanager, I have set up a Website keyed to the chapters of this book. Web technologies are constantly developing and changing, and you will always be able to find up-to-date and reliable information about the Web and Web resources at the *Web Works* Website. All links to Web and Net materials cited in the book will be found there, as well as links to carefully selected examples of materials covered in each chapter. Look for the Website icon, which indicates places where you can go to find further information, links to Websites mentioned in the book, and updates to material covered.

The Website will thus allow new users to try out the features of the Web described in the book and will provide more experienced users with a convenient jump station for quick access to research tools and guides to information. There is also a user comment form so that you can provide suggestions for additions or corrections. Users who provide tips will be acknowledged in additions to the Website and in future editions of *Web Works*.

Platforms and Software Reference Points

Web Works is written with the Microsoft Windows user in mind, although most descriptions of software features will also include references to Macintosh versions. Most software features are identical in the main graphical interface platforms—Windows, Mac, and X-Windows—although the menu system or commands for using the features may vary slightly.

I have chosen *Netscape Navigator* as the reference World Wide Web client program for several reasons. (*Netscape Navigator* 2.0 will be assumed throughout this book. The program features of Netscape 2.0 have been continued in version 3.0.) Netscape Communications Corporation has done more than any other company to advance the multimedia potential of the Web and continues to make the free educational use of their products a part of their corporate philosophy. I strongly endorse Netscape's model of synergy with educational and research institutions and hope it spreads. But since this book focuses on Web and networked computing concepts rather than on the features of any one piece of hardware or software, most of what you will find explained using Netscape as a reference point will be true for any other recent graphical Web client program (like NCSA *Mosaic* or Microsoft *Internet Explorer*).

Web References

References to Websites mentioned in this book are reliable as this book goes to press. Some URLs may change, and linkrot—the inevitable decay of Web links in a dynamic, constantly changing distributed system—will set in for some references. To stay current with the ongoing development of the Web, use the *Web Works* Website for updates on all the information cited in this book.

Acknowledgments

Deborah Everhart, my sine qua non and favorite Webmistress, has read every word at each stage from first draft to finished typescript and has provided indispensible suggestions and criticism. She also contributed material for Chapters 5 and 8 and a section each of Chapters 4 and 7. Our Web work has always been collaborative, and this book, our first publishing venture outside Webspace, would be a far lesser product without the interweaving of Deborah's Internet experience and editing sense.

I'm also grateful to Laura LaBauve, our Labyrinth project intern, and Kate Forte, of Georgetown University's Academic Computing Services, for reading a draft of the book and offering valuable comments and suggestions.

I've had many hours of collegial conversation with Randy Bass, my co-conspirator at Georgetown, and though he probably won't recognize it, his insights on hypermedia and misgivings about the current state of the Web have informed my thinking and even tempered my Web evangelism.

I'm thankful for the valuable comments and suggestions provided by my readers, James Ross, Anne Woodlief, and Bill Newmiller, and for insights and corrections from Stephen King at W. W. Norton. Many thanks to others at Norton who have helped out: Marian Johnson, Kurt Wildermuth, Diane O'Connor, Warren Johnson, and Kristin Sheerin. A special word of thanks must go to Carol Hollar-Zwick, my editor, who has helped with every stage of the book and provided excellent editorial advice for every chapter.

Introduction

I have said on numerous occasions, and I still believe, that with the development of the Internet, and with the increasing pervasiveness of communication between networked computers, we are in the middle of the most transforming technological event since the capture of fire. I used to think that it was just the biggest thing since Gutenberg, but now I think you have to go back farther.

—John Perry Barlow, co-founder of the Electronic Freedom Foundation, former lyricist for the Grateful Dead

Over the past three decades, worldwide communications and information exchange have undergone a two-part quiet revolution: in 1969 the first "internet" was tested at UCLA, and in 1991 the World Wide Web was launched at the CERN particle physics lab in Geneva. The Internet has grown from 23 host computers in 1971 to over 9.5 million in 96 countries in 1996. But this revolution is unlike anything else our planet has seen since the invention of the technology for recording, storing, and transporting words, numbers, and images on clay tablets. The Web is global and interactive, and users or consumers of information can also become producers and publishers. Barlow is right—it's a bigger transformation than Gutenberg's press, and we are experiencing the broad social effects of the new communications environment in the course of a single generation. This book is for people who want to enter this new communications environment and understand how it works.

This is also a book that presents a distinctive approach to *usable* technology for people who are not technical. *Web Works* attempts to dispel some of the anxieties about technology that prevent smart people from taking advantage of access to information that will greatly assist them in their work and from enjoying the benefits of participating in a wider community of people with like interests. People learning to use the Net and Web in the 1990s bring a lot of contemporary social baggage to their computers, and learning the Web, like learning other socially-embedded things, may require unlearning a lot of what we think we know.

Our culture is based on incompatible ways of dealing with new technology, formed of equal parts hype, worship, fear, and distrust. The past decade has seen escalating cyberhype, promises of new techno-utopias, plans for information superhighways, dreams of new educational achievement through computers, and large investments in technology by businesses seeking greater productivity and profits. On another front, the popular media seems fixated by the fantasy that the Net is a big scary place full of mischievous hackers, cyberthieves, porn pushers, and computer security leaks as big as Niagara Falls.

Fantasies are extremely difficult to resist with something as weak as facts and experience. The simple truth that the Net fills ordinary human needs like the need for communication over distances and the need for access to reliable, usable information is too banal for headlines. There are many social concerns that the Net community and technology architects need to address, but the Web is still a new and developing technology with a long way to go. Our computers are only as smart as we are. But as you learn the Web from the inside, you'll soon find yourself unlearning some popular misconceptions about technology. The information and communication environment you'll discover will soon seem habitable, and you'll even want to live and build your own place there.

Learning the Web with the *Web Works* Approach

This book takes the approach that all Web users will get the most out of the Web if they know some of the basics about how it works. You might ask, why bother learning how things work as long as the computer does pretty much what I want it to do? Here's why. The World Wide Web is unlike any other electronic medium in its user orientation. Unlike TV or radio, the Web user is in charge of the information requested and received. Broadcast media simply bombards us with simultaneous multiple channels. We have no control over the delivery of content on a TV channel; there's nothing on TV to help us evaluate or interpret the content of one channel or another. You can't ask a TV program to back up or compare one segment of content to something earlier or later. Our only choices are changing the channel or turning off the TV.

The Web is actually the inverse of broadcast media: the Web user initiates the search for interesting or useful content, and the information is delivered on request to a user's computer. Since information is requested and not broadcast, Web users make direct decisions about quality, content, reliability, relevance, and connectedness. Unlike the TV viewer, the Web user can evaluate, analyze, and interpret the information brought to the computer screen and compare it, almost instantly, with other information. With the ability to compare information from multiple media sources quickly and by request, the Web user can efficiently convert the information into usable knowledge.

And there's more: Web users can become producers of information. No other medium allows consumer access to the means of production like the Web. As you learn the Web, you will quickly find that you can become a developer and producer of information, and not simply a receiver or consumer. Placing the user as close to the means of production as possible has always been a key feature of Internet technology and Net culture.

Is the Web Worth Learning? Some Examples

OK, all this may seem intriguing so far, but how can you tell if learning to use the Web will be worth it for you? How could having access to information on the Net help with practical, daily needs and concerns? Let's look at a few examples.

1. Travel

You've always wanted to visit Prague, but you don't have any idea where to find the information you need to prepare for a trip. You could go to a bookstore or call a travel agent, but you could also do a quick search for "Prague" on the Web. Here's what you'd find in about a minute or two. First, there's an encyclopedia of information hosted by the city of Prague itself, including a history of the city and information for visitors. There's a virtual tour of the city provided by a Prague university, information on Prague hotels, and even information about Prague radio broadcasts in English. You can find a history of the Czech Republic, and all kinds of cultural and business information. Maybe you need to do some research while in Prague. Information about Prague's library and access to library catalogs are available on the Net. What airlines fly to Prague and what are their flight schedules? Check the travel and airline Websites; many are being added weekly. All up to date, all freely accessible on the Web. Now call the travel agent (many of them are on the Web, too).*

***Hint:** Use the search engines and World Wide Web Virtual Library site discussed in Chapter 4.

2. Research

You have a research topic and need solid information and a working bibliography for a paper, report, or article. You've also got a deadline. How to begin? You could spend hours with print indices, bibliographies, library card catalogs, or reference books. Instead, you could use some of the Web indices and search engines described in Chapter 4. It's likely that someone, or a whole organization, has put information on your topic on the Web. Next, use an online library catalog (see 4.5, page 66). There are over 3,000 publicly accessible library catalogs on the Net, including all the major university research libraries and many large city libraries. (The Net and Web are not antibook; but we no longer need to use print sources to study or research books.) The online catalogs allow you to search by author, title, or subject, and you can compile a working bibliography in a very short amount of time. Need journal references? The Net also has a searchable online database of thousands of journals and tables of contents. An hour of research using Web and Net materials can result in (1) a list of Websites with the most up-to-date information on your topic, (2) a bibliography of titles that you need to investigate, and (3) some key journal articles that you can look up. Having prepared your research, you can now visit your library to investigate the print materials and not waste any time when you get there. It's no exaggeration to say that with Web access you can do in an hour what it used to take a week or more to do with print indices, card catalogs, and other physically limited research aids.

3. News

OK, say you've now got your new notebook computer with a zippy internal modem and a new account with a national Internet provider. You travel frequently, and you want to keep up on news and information in your field and stay connected with friends and colleagues via email. (Make sure you book hotels that allow you to jack in your modem to the phone line in your room!) Forget trying to get the news you need from local newspapers. It's all on the Web. The *CNN Interactive* Website is great (updated continuously throughout the day), and the *New York Times* and *Wall Street Journal* have Web editions that contain not only the current day's news but a searchable archive of recent stories. Many Web editions of newspapers and magazines have complete archives covering several years. Some Web editions require a (usually free) registration, others a small subscription fee. You can also get free stock and mutual funds quotes 24 hours a day on the Web from wherever you are. The news is always available, even late at night when you've just returned to the hotel. Leave the TV off; there's more on the Web.

These are only a few typical examples of how learning the Web can change the way you use and access information. Internet content and accessibility have now achieved critical mass: nontechnical people in all fields and careers now have easy and reliable access to information when they need it. Internet technology will continue to evolve with better user software and new delivery of media, but any investment of time you make in learning the Web with *Web Works* now will enable you to learn further on your own and prepare you for new advances in Net and Web technology.

1 The Internet and World Wide Web: What It Is and How It Works

The standard answer to the question "What is the Internet?" is usually "The global network of computer networks." That's true enough, but it's too general to explain what makes the Internet (or Net) work or what distinguishes it from a commercial online service like CompuServe, America Online (AOL), or Lexis/Nexis. In some popular media discussions, computers, networks, and dial-up services via a modem are all confusingly called the "Internet" or "cyberspace." The Internet and World Wide Web are sometimes treated as two separate systems rather than as developments of the same technology. We're often told that we live in the Information Age, but finding straight and accurate information about the Net in the popular media can be absurdly difficult. Let's start with the basics.

1.1 What Is the Internet?

There are three components that make the Internet what it is today:

- The Net as a worldwide computer system using a common means for linking hardware and transmitting digital information.
- The Net as a community of people using a common communications technology.
- The Net as a globally distributed system of information.

In practical and functional terms, the Internet is

- A 24-hour nonstop global forum and communications system.
- An online library and international information system.
- A business and corporate communications medium.
- A distance learning and remote education system.
- A commercial transactions medium.

- A multimedia delivery system for news and entertainment.
- A government information service.
- All of the above simultaneously.

Since the Net allows the transmission of any content in any medium that we now have the means to digitize, it is quite simply the best information and communications system ever invented. It often appears anarchic and disorganized, but this is part of its openness. And unlike network or cable TV, it is user centered, allowing more human agency in communications and information exchange than ever before. The Net is interactive by design, meaning that decisions about use and content lie more with users than with producers. But since the Net has user access built into the medium, any user with a minimal amount of training can also become a producer of information. Furthermore, with graphical interfaces to the Net like *Netscape Navigator,* the complex architecture of the Internet system itself is rendered almost invisible, so that we can focus on the content and benefit from the interactivity.

The Net is a whole information environment for various communities of people. Contrary to some media coverage of the Net and Web, the Net doesn't isolate people; it connects them to a larger world outside their own experience. For this reason, we can't simply isolate the computer network either from the human agents who use and develop it or from the content, the information, which this network makes it possible to transmit and use.

The Net has helped create the electronic "global village" that Marshall McLuhan and others imagined in the late 1960s. With a simple mouse click, anyone using the World Wide Web can access information from across the world more quickly than it takes a TV set to warm up. But as citizens in this interconnected world, we can't usefully separate out the computer architecture—the physical hardware and ways of transmitting digital electronic signals—from the global information resources or from the human lives shaped by the medium and by new access to information and communication. In practical, everyday terms, the Net for most people *is* the readily accessible information and the open communications with others.

1.2 Where Did the Net and Web Come From?

The Internet is an amazingly self-documenting system, containing many files of information on the history and development of networking and communications technology. No other communications technology has ever been developed in which information about how the technology works is built into the system.

In brief, the Internet is the result of computer research developed in the late 1960s by the Defense Department's Advanced Research Projects Agency (ARPA), and the first internetworked system was called ARPANET. But don't imagine scenes out of *Dr. Strangelove* or *1984*. The ARPA research team was a group of university-trained computer engineers with an interesting problem to solve, one that would have broad social benefits. The problem was how to network government computers so that they could withstand an attack and continue to exchange data reliably, even if parts of the network were unreliable. How could a network be created with no single point of failure, no central hub, that could be disabled by a nuclear attack? It was a basic problem—reliable networked data exchange—and they had an elegant solution.

The Internet as we know it today derives from the solution to the ARPA problem proposed by Vinton Cerf and Robert Kahn in the early 1970s. The Internet concept solved the broken network problem through a three-part solution. The Internet model consists of (1) a network system with multiple routes of transmission, (2) a method for transmitting information in chunks called "packets" rather than in a steady stream, and (3) common ways of linking incompatible hardware through rules that all computers can follow. The Internet was thus born from the set of networking protocols—rules for transmitting and receiving data that don't depend on the hardware type—developed by Cerf, Kahn, and other computer scientists for an efficient and reliable way to exchange data between networked computers.

The first "internet" based on ARPA models was simply four experimental computers (network "nodes") networked from UCLA in September 1969. Other research centers and universities were linked with Internet protocols during the late 1970s and early 1980s. The Internet has grown from 23 "host" computers (the servers on the network) in 1971 to over 9.5 million in 96 countries as of the first quarter of 1996. As the need for networking grew in the United States during the 1980s, the National Science Foundation formed the NSFNet in 1987, the national network that linked all the regional networks using Internet protocols. In 1987 there were just over 28,000 Internet host computers, and the Internet was also opened to other countries around the world. Internet standards and connectivity now extend to educational and research institutions; every branch of federal, state, and local governments; and commercial and nonprofit organizations.[1]

By 1997, there will be 10 million host computers on the Internet in around 100 countries. No one is really certain about the number of worldwide users of the Internet (at least 50 million), since there are many ways of gaining access and multiple users for any host system.[2] One of the interesting historical ironies about the Net is that what began as a Cold War technology is now open to millions of people around the world, including countries that were formerly Cold War enemies of the United States and the West. The Internet solution for an efficient, reliable network is now a global project for worldwide communications.

The World Wide Web uses the Internet for delivering information in the hypertext and hypermedia format. The Web was founded at CERN, the European particle physics lab in Geneva, Switzerland, by Tim Berners-Lee in 1989 and opened to world access in 1991. CERN has ended its official involvement in the development of the Web, and now Berners-Lee heads the W3 Consortium at MIT, the group that coordinates the development of the Web. The Web's graphical interface and hypermedia capability accounts for most of the great expansion of the Internet since 1993 (see Chapter 2).

1.3 How Does the Net Work?

The goal of good computer interface design has always been making complex operations seem transparent to the user, and

1. Statistics are from the Internet Society (**http://www.isoc.org**), Hobbes' Internet Time Line (**http://info.isoc.org/guest/zakon/Internet/History/HIT.html**), and the Internet Domain Survey (**http://www.nw.com/zone/WWW/top.html**). For other sites with reliable Internet statistics and demographics, see **http://www.yahoo.com/Computers_and_Internet/Internet/Statistics-and-Demographics/** For a useful overview of Internet history in a print journal, see Jeffrey A. Hart, Robert R. Reed, and François Bar, "The Building of the Internet," *Telecommunications Policy* (Nov. 1992): 666–89.

2. Estimates of worldwide users range from 50 to 300 million. There were over 37 million users in the United States by the end of 1995, and that figure is now much larger, since most proprietary online services like AOL and CompuServe now provide Internet access. For stats as they become available, see the Internet Index (**http://www.openmarket.com/intindex/**) and the sites listed in note 1 above.

this is as it should be. Recent Web software makes navigating the Web and finding information easy and fairly transparent. But the ease of transparency can slide over into ignorant mystification or mistrust. The user-centeredness of the Net requires us to demystify the technology and understand a few of its essential features.

Internet technology is about moving bits efficiently from computer to computer across a network. There are a few key principles that make the Internet work, and even those of us who have no technical background in computers can grasp the concepts and watch how they work.

There are several layers to the networking technology that help move our bits from one computer to another. Let's begin with the first four: (1) the kind of network that the Internet is; (2) the data transmission methods, "protocols" in Netspeak, for bouncing bits across this network so that they arrive at the right place; (3) the architecture or systems design that allows computers of all types to interact with each other across a network, and (4) the common protocols for files and email that Net users encounter.

The Packet-switching Network Concept

The foundational principle of the Internet is what is called the "packet-switching" network. We are familiar with using one kind of electronic communications network every day—the telephone system. Standard telephone technology, however, uses what's called a "circuit-switching" network. When you make a phone call, a point-to-point dedicated signal path is made across a network of phone lines and signal switches, and as long as you're on the line, the network provides a straight-through connection between your phone and the phone at the other end. The cliché "hold the line" isn't just a metaphor. (Of course, telephone companies now use satellite and even digital transmission at points along the way, but your phone call still needs a dedicated path in the network.)

The Internet doesn't use this dedicated signal-path method. The packet-switching network uses a transmission method that breaks up the data files we send and receive into smaller chunks called data packets. (Actually, there is a set of protocols known as TCP/IP that does the work of the network; more on this later.) Instead of being sent to a destination point like a phone call on a dedicated path, the packets of digital data have Internet addresses attached to them and are routed to their destination in the Net by their addresses. It would be a very inefficient use of a computer network with millions of computers if every transmission required a dedicated connection that had to be held open like a phone call. Instead, the packets can take various routes to their receiving addresses, and no individual transmission can tie up the network. The Internet packet network is designed for efficiency and speed: packets can be rerouted through the system to achieve the most efficient delivery.

It's useful to think of an Internet packet as a datagram with a digital wrapper or envelope: the datagram's wrapper includes information about the address of the sending and receiving computers, the size of the datagram, and the order of the separate datagrams so that the whole file can be recombined and displayed on the receiving end. At any moment in the Net, there are millions of packets bouncing around on their way to a Net destination. This means that an email message you send or a Web file you access doesn't get sent out like a telephone call but like a series of digital chunks. Your Net files and messages don't flow in a steady, unbroken stream of bits like water through a pipe, but are broken up into packets that share the network with everyone else's packets.

It's important to grasp that an Internet packet isn't a complete document like a letter enclosed in an envelope but a portion of a larger file. There could be thousands of packets in the data stream between the first and second packet in that email message you just sent. But because all these data transmissions happen in microseconds behind the scenes, we don't really notice. In a sense, you could say everyone's packets are created equal, and everyone shares the resources of the Net as a worldwide system.

Internet Protocols

How do the packets get transmitted and how do they reach their destination? This is where the TCP/IP protocols and the network routers come in. *TCP/IP* stands for Transmission Control Protocol/Internet Protocol, and these protocols are often simply called IP. A protocol in communications technology is a rule for transmitting data by means of electronic instructions carried with the data. For example, signals must be sent and rules followed to get your printer to print out that stream of bits we think of as a text file or to get a computer on the Internet to interpret an incoming burst of bits from the network. A protocol, then, isn't part of the content of a data file, but instructions that tell the computer what to do with the data.

TCP/IP are the two main layers of protocols that send packets on their way and make sure they end up where they're sent. It's easiest to think of these protocols as providing two envelopes for a data packet. Internet Protocol (IP) takes care of addressing the packets and providing the information for routing them on their way. IP works with all the network routers, the dedicated computers on a network that simply read IP addresses and send the packets through to the best network connection. Packets generally go through many routers between sending and receiving computers. Transmission Control Protocol (TCP) works to control the size, order, and type of the packets themselves. On the sending end, TCP software takes the data you want to send and breaks them into packets. Each packet gets wrapped in an envelope that contains the packet number, size of the packet, and total file size. On the receiving end, TCP software collects the packets, puts them in the proper order, and checks to see that they are complete. When all goes well, all this happens behind the scenes in a New York minute.

So, the real answer to the question "What is the Internet?" is the network of computers using the suite of TCP/IP protocols for moving bits. If a computer doesn't have an IP address and doesn't use Internet protocols, it is not "on the Internet."

Client–Server Architecture

There's one final piece to the Internet model of computing, and it accounts for the way your computer interacts with the other computers on the Net. This is the "client–server" structure. The Net and Web software on your own PC or workstation is called the "client" software since it makes requests of another computer running "server" software. In Netspeak, servers serve files to clients. The computers on the Net that store the files and information are known as "servers" or "hosts." And here's where the IP addresses come in again: if your computer is connected to the Internet, it has an IP address known by your client software like Netscape, which interacts with the host systems or servers on the Net by their IP addresses.

Here's what happens behind the scenes of a client–server process:

1. You click on a hotlink or use another command for an Internet process.

2. Your client software makes a request of a server by sending it to the server's IP address.
3. The server responds by sending the files, which are routed and delivered to your address.
4. Your software interprets the incoming files and displays them on your screen.

All this in a matter of milliseconds.

The client–server architecture is very efficient. Computing power and information are distributed throughout the system and not concentrated at a central point. A client–server system also means that much of the work of the Internet is done locally, on the client side, at the actual interface with the user. A user interacts with a server only for a brief amount of time, the time it takes for a server to respond to a client request; a user can use the information received from a server for an unlimited amount of time with software on the user's local computer. Client programs for the Net and Web will get increasingly smarter, focusing on user-defined features for searching, displaying, and interpreting information stored on the servers.

Client–Server Protocols for Moving Bits on the Internet

While TCP/IP does the basic work of data transmission and traffic flow on the Internet, there are also protocols for file delivery and accessing other computers that require specific types of client–server interaction. Beginning Net users will encounter four basic types of protocols as soon as they get on the Net.

PROTOCOLS FOR MOVING FILES BETWEEN INTERNET SERVERS AND USERS' COMPUTERS

FTP: File Transfer Protocol

FTP is used for uploading and downloading files between computers on the Internet. Of course, uploading files to a server can be done only when a user has permission to use space on a server, either through a user account or in a directory open to "anonymous" (that is, guest) users. All file types (text, graphics, audio, video, binary programs) can be transferred with this protocol.

There are many practical purposes for FTP. You can upload a file to your user directory on the server you use for email and send the file as an email message or attachment. You can download software from a server and install it on your own computer. And there are still millions of publicly accessible files on anonymous FTP servers around the world, though many of these files have migrated to Web servers. FTP is built into Web client software like Netscape, and Netscape will display many types of files served from FTP servers (for example, plain text or image files).

Gopher

The Gopher file protocol uses a menu system for delivering files from servers to users' client systems. "Gopher" gets its name from its originators at the University of Minnesota (home of the Golden Gophers), and from its obvious utility as a file fetcher (as in it "goes fer" files). Gopher is file delivery only, no uploading; and is mainly used for delivering text files, though all file types can be transferred. Most of the files developed earlier for Gopher delivery have been redesigned as Web files. Gopher still provides quick delivery and easy access to plain text files, though these cannot be hyperlinked like Web documents.

The Gopher protocol likewise is built into Netscape and other Web client software. Netscape will fetch and display most types of files from Gopher servers, though the vast majority of Gopher files will be plain text.

World Wide Web—HTTP: Hypertext Transport Protocol

The Web uses a special protocol for delivering files in the hypertext and hypermedia format. All file types are supported, and, like Gopher, file transmission is from servers to users' local computers. The user's local computer runs a Web client program like Netscape, which makes requests of the server, receives the incoming files, and displays them on the screen. When someone mentions a "Web server" or "Website," they are referring to an HTTP server on the Internet.

This is the main protocol that Netscape and other Web client software is designed to use. Interacting with HTTP servers, Netscape requests hypermedia files and then displays or plays them.

PROTOCOL FOR DELIVERING INTERNET EMAIL—SMTP: SIMPLE MAIL TRANSFER PROTOCOL SMTP is the protocol that Internet mail servers use for sending, passing on, and processing Internet email. It may not be as visible to Net users as the file protocols discussed above, but we all depend on it for sending and receiving email.

PROTOCOL FOR DELIVERING USENET NEWSGROUP MAIL—NNTP: NETWORK NEWS TRANSPORT PROTOCOL NNTP is used for delivering Usenet Newsgroup (discussion group) postings to Usenet servers. Messages are posted electronically to a central bulletin board system. Users read and respond to messages that they access from an NNTP server by using a Usenet reader (a client program that interacts with the NNTP server). *Netscape Navigator* has a built-in newsreader. Most institutional Internet servers like those at universities or Internet service providers also host Usenet Newsgroups.

PROTOCOL FOR REMOTE LOGIN TO ANOTHER COMPUTER ON THE INTERNET: TELNET Telnet is a protocol for using a remote server or host system from somewhere else on the Net. Technically speaking, telnet is an Internet protocol for remote "terminal emulation," which means a way to get a computer to act like a terminal for another computer across the Internet. To run a telnet session, you must be able to login to the remote computer, either with a protected username and password or with a public access or guest login.

A telnet connection is also necessary for linking to an IRC (Internet Relay Chat) server and to most MUDs and MOOs on the Net. Telnet also works with *Netscape Navigator* as a helper application. You will also find special client software for IRC and MUDs, but these are versions of telnet configured for these applications.

We will need to return to the function of these protocols later. At this point, it's important to know what the basic Internet protocols are and what they do.

1.4 What Is the World Wide Web?

The Web is the Net's interactive multimedia delivery system. The Internet is about moving bits efficiently and reliably across a large network, and the World Wide Web expands on this principle by creating a uniform way of delivering and displaying digital information.

Here's a complete definition: the World Wide Web is a globally distributed, dynamic, hypermedia system on the Internet. Let's unpack this definition a bit. The Web is global in the sense that it includes Web servers and client computers around the world. It is a distributed system, meaning that information resources are found dispersed throughout the network and not centralized on one or even a few computers. It is dynamic, meaning that the contents are constantly changing, growing, and developing. Its distinguishing feature is the use of hypertext and hypermedia, meaning that no document is an island, but can be configured to link to many other documents and files in any digital medium (text, image, video, sound).

The Web uses a special Internet protocol known as HTTP (Hypertext Transport Protocol), for delivering hypertext and hypermedia documents across the Net. Like all Internet protocols, the Web is based on the client–server system: your Web browser or client program makes a file request of a Web server, which runs the HTTP software; the file is delivered to your Net address; and your client displays the file. The Web was also designed to be backwardly or downwardly compatible with existing Internet protocols and file transfer systems like Gopher and FTP. You may often find links to Gopher and FTP files in Web documents, and most of the time the links simply work transparently. The Web is based on the same open-systems standards as the Net but creates a different result for the Web user—an integrated, globally distributed system of information that works transparently.

1.5 What Isn't the Internet?

The popular media often refer to all computer networking as "cyberspace" or the "Internet," and there's still more noise than signal out there when it comes to accurate information about the Net and Web. (Remember *Time* magazine's cyberporn scare?) Let's get one thing straight: all networks, dial-up online services, or Bulletin Board Systems (BBSs) that use proprietary connections rather than Internet protocols are *not* the Internet. Any computer system not assigned an IP address and not connected to an Internet router isn't part of the Internet. This doesn't mean that local, proprietary, or commercial services like a BBS or online service aren't useful or sophisticated systems; it simply means that they are not part of the Internet.

Commercial online services like America Online (AOL) and CompuServe use a proprietary interface and data protocols that provide closed proprietary content to their subscribers. Although these online services provide an Internet "gateway" (a connecting link between incompatible systems) for email and now also provide access to the Web, they do not use IP protocols or open standards for their modem communications with their customers. This is important information for Internet users: Net and Web access will always be slower through these proprietary gateways than through a direct Internet connection, because the data needs to be translated for the proprietary system.

As demand for the Web exploded in 1995, AOL and CompuServe saw that they needed to provide access to the Web for their customers. (Web access also provided these commercial services with instant, free content, since Web resources were already out there and did not require new content development on their part.) Commercial proprietary networks begun by AT&T and Microsoft converted to the Internet early in 1996, since the demand for Net access was enormous. Online services are constantly changing, and AOL now has an Internet-only service, GNN (Global Network Navigator). Proprietary online services that don't provide Internet access no longer seem viable. No commercial service can hope to duplicate the openly accessible worldwide content of the Web.

1.6 Who Owns the Net and the Web?

Internet technology is nonproprietary (no one can own it), and the technical specifications needed for developing software and hardware for the Internet are freely available. The physical communications links for the Net are worldwide telecommunications lines. This means no one—no individual, government, or corporation—actually "owns" the Internet in the sense of owning property or a trademark, but all countries linked by the Net own pieces of it in that telecommunications companies, governments, and other organizations own the data lines, switches, and routers that make up the network. All countries on the Net, therefore, "own" it by supplying the dedicated lines that transmit the data.

In the United States, the main high-speed "backbone" linking all the regional networks was initially developed and maintained by the National Science Foundation in 1987. This backbone was privatized in 1995 and is now maintained by U.S. telecommunications companies.

By keeping the system and the standards open, everyone can benefit. During 1995–1996, most of the key industry players that contribute to the growth of networked technology embraced and promoted the cross-platform, open standards principle of the Net and Web. Why? Because the open system means everyone can compete to develop products that will work on the Internet regardless of the user's equipment. There's a beautiful paradox: everyone profits by not owning the Internet and by not making proprietary products.

1.7 Who Runs the Net and the Web?

Since no one owns or governs the Net, there is a need for agreed-on standards and protocols for the international network to work. Although not a law-making or governing body, the Internet Society, which has its physical headquarters in Reston, Virginia, establishes policy and global standards for Internetworking around the world:

> The Internet Society is a non-governmental International organization for global cooperation and coordination for the Internet and its internetworking technologies and applications.
>
> The Society's individual and organizational members are bound by a common stake in maintaining the viability and global scaling of the Internet. They comprise the companies, government agencies, and foundations that have created the Internet and its technologies as well as innovative new entrepreneurial organizations contributing to maintain that dynamic (**http://info.isoc.org/whatis/index.html**).

The main group responsible for Internet working protocols is the IAB, (Internet Architecture Board), and the IETF (Internet Engineering Task Force), a consortium of computer networking specialists who research ways to develop Internet technology.

The Internet Society's Website contains useful online articles about the history of the Internet and graphs that map the growth and development of the Net and Web around the world. Many other Websites host a wide array of information about the Net and how it works, and the most up-to-date information about the Net will always be on the Net.

The World Wide Web Consortium (W3 Consortium), founded and directed by the Web's inventor, Tim Berners-Lee, helps coordinate standards, protocols, and applications for the Web in ways similar to the Internet Society. The W3 Consortium Website is always a good place to visit to watch new developments in Web resources and technology, and you don't need to be a computer expert to appreciate the work of these dedicated Websters.

1.8 Who Pays for the Internet?

In North America, universities, businesses, organizations, governments, and individuals pay for use of the Internet. This model of telecommunications access and marketing is increasingly being followed around the world, but other countries have different regulations for Internet access and ways of paying for it.

For practical purposes, there are two ways of paying: as a group (an organization or institution with many networked computer users) or as an individual (a single user paying for Internet access, ordinarily via a modem connection). The Net uses dedicated, high-speed data lines that telecommunications companies price out in various ways. Everyone pays a little for their own small piece of the Net so that no one has to pay a lot.

Access to the Internet is usually provided by telecommunications companies that buy, install, and maintain the lines and hardware that provide the data links to and among the servers on the Net. Large institutions like universities, for example, usually pay a local telephone company for a high-speed data connection to the regional network connected to the Internet. Many corporations and other organizations do the same. With institutional access to the Net, the direct cost to employees or students is usually little or nothing because Internet access becomes part of the operating expenses of the institution or corporation.

Individuals can pay for access to the Net by using an Internet Service Provider (ISP). The ISP business has become a growth industry, and the recent Telecommunications Reform Act will make Internet services very competitive. An ISP can provide various kinds of Net connectivity, ranging from modem access over ordinary phone lines to high-speed, dedicated data lines linked straight to an office Local Area Network (LAN). Individual users pay for an account on an Internet server maintained by the ISP, which has purchased or leased the networking hardware (modems and routers) and high-speed data lines connected to the Net (see Chapter 3).

1.9 Digital Nuts and Bolts: What's in an Internet Address?

If you already use Internet email, you're familiar with some of the basics of an Internet address. But there's more involved behind the scenes, and to use the Web intelligently, it's useful to know what Internet addresses mean.

There's a lot of information in an Internet address, but most of it is for us humans operating with wetware (brain memory).

Let's start with an example of an email address:

There are two halves to an email address, each part separated by the @ sign: the username and the Internet computer name (known as the "host name" or "server name") and domain name. In this example, *president* is the name of a user on the system known as *whitehouse.gov* (spoken as "whitehouse dot gov").

The Internet host name after the @ sign contains other information—the name assigned to the computer system itself (whitehouse) and the Internet domain (gov). Yes, there really is a computer on the Net called "whitehouse" (but it's not physically at the White House).

The Domain Name System

Computers on the Internet are organized by what is known as the Domain Name System (DNS). In Netspeak, "domains" are broad categories of use that make it easier to administer and remember the variety of computer systems that make up the Net. Although there is no central government for the Net, guidelines for domain names and a central registration service for assigning names to Internet computers is provided by the InterNIC (Internet Network Information Center).

To read a Net address, begin at the end, at what is known as the "top level" domain, which appears as the final abbreviation at the end of an address. The DNS started in the United States, the original home of the Internet, and then expanded to other countries. In the United States, there are six top-level domains for different types of organizations:

.edu	Educational and research organizations
.com	Commercial (business) organizations
.gov	Government nonmilitary organizations
.mil	U.S. military branches
.org	Nonprofit organizations
.net	Network organizations, network access providers

When the Internet expanded to other countries, each nation was assigned a top-level domain in a two-letter abbreviation, usually an abbreviation of the country name in the country's national language or accepted usage (for example, Germany is ".de" for Deutschland).

The Internet also allows for subdomains, which are names registered by institutions and organizations for all Internetworked computers administered within that organization. For example, there are many computers on the Net at my university, Georgetown, and they all use the Georgetown subdomain name with .edu, the top-level domain:

INFORMATION SITE 1

NET BASICS

Site	URL
On the history of the Net	**gopher://gopher.isoc.org/11/internet/history/**
Internet Timeline	**http://info.isoc.org/guest/zakon/Internet/History/HIT.html**
Daedalus's Guide to the Web	**http://www.georgetown.edu/labyrinth/general/general.html**
Information about the Internet (Library of Congress)	**http://www.loc.gov/global/internet/internet.html**
Internet Demographics and Statistics	**http://www.yahoo.com/Computers_and_Internet/Internet/Statistics_and_Demographics/**
Internet Society (ISOC)	**http://info.isoc.org/**
ISOC FAQ	**http://info.isoc.org/whatis/what-is-isoc.html**
CERN	**http://www.cern.ch/**
The World Wide Web (W3) Consortium	**http://www.w3.org/pub/WWW/**
The WWW Project (W3 Consortium)	**http://www.w3.org/hypertext/WWW/TheProject.html**
The Internet Network Information Center (InterNIC)	**http://www.internic.net/**

"physics.georgetown.edu," "www.georgetown.edu," and "gusun.georgetown.edu" are all computers maintained on the Georgetown network by our Internet administrators. Here's an example of a server name that uses the subdomain system:

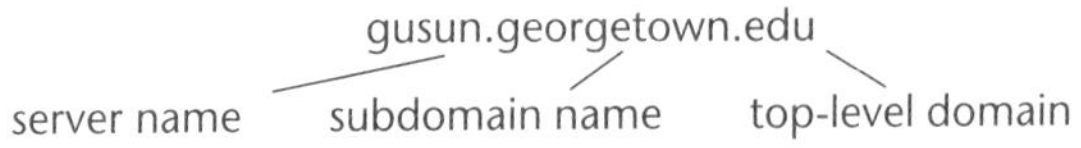

gusun.georgetown.edu

server name — subdomain name — top-level domain

Most universities and large organizations with multiple servers use the subdomain name system for their various servers.

Domain Name Servers: Numeric Address Translators

But these alphabetical addresses are really just nicknames for us brain-memory humans to use. Computers on the Net know the unique addresses of Internet servers by numerical addresses. Hence the need for the Domain Name System and the array of DNS servers all over the Internet that match names with numerical addresses. Internet systems administrators associate a numerical address (known as the IP address) with a name for each server. (Names and associated IP addresses have to be registered with InterNIC so that there are no duplicates.) When you access a file from a Website, send email, or use any other Internet protocol, a DNS server used by your region of the Net translates the letters and abbreviations in an address to a numerical address. (whitehouse.gov, for example, is 198.137.241.30, but who would want to remember that?)

The DNS also allows for "aliases" or multiple names to be assigned to one computer. For example, you can get the Library of Congress's Web server by typing in **www.loc.gov** or **lcweb.lc.gov**—both names are aliases for the same numerical Internet address (140.147.248.7).

The DNS is like a library call number system: we know books by titles and authors, but the unique location for a book in relation to all the other books is most easily managed by coded call numbers. To find a book in a library, we need to look up the call number. Domain Name Servers look up names and automatically translate them into IP addresses. The main Internet servers, which store and deliver data, are constantly communicating with the name servers, allowing the main servers to send out data packets to the specified addresses. Of course, if you find out the IP address of the Internet computer you want to access, you can use the numerical address and bypass the DNS. (This is sometimes useful if a name server is temporarily down.) But remembering IP addresses is about as easy or useful as remembering call numbers for library books.

1.10 Intranets: Internet Islands

Over the past few years, businesses, universities, and other organizations have found that Internet and Web technology is also an efficient way of setting up and delivering information through a local or secure network. Internetworking, while a global standard for worldwide communications, also works in a LAN or a secure password-protected network, sometimes called an Intranet.

For example, a university can set up a licensed or limited-access database accessible via a Web client like Netscape but served through a closed, campuswide network. Everyone has access to the information freely on the campus, but the database is not accessible to the whole world. Similarly, businesses and government agencies are setting up intranets using Net and Web technology for delivering sensitive or secure information within a network that is only accessible to a limited or authorized group of users. The People's Republic of China is reportedly wiring the country as an Intranet, using TCP/IP protocols for intracountry communications, but greatly restricting access in and out of the national network.

Although a seeming contradiction to the open global networking concept, an Intranet using TCP/IP and Web client–server software is actually a very inexpensive and efficient way of serving large amounts of information to users within a secure or private network. We'll see more LANs and secure network systems operating this way in the future, and your institution or organization may already be using an Intranet for some purposes.

2

Web Basics: Key Concepts for World Wide Web Users

It's much easier to become a World Wide Web information manager once you understand a few of the central features of the Web. The Web's user-orientation and open standards make the key features very accessible. The important point is to gain a basic grasp of the main concepts that drive the technology.

2.1 The Network Is Your Computer: Out of the Box, into the Net

It makes a big difference whether we conceive of our computers as closed boxes or as access points to a network. Bill Gates of Microsoft dreamed of a country with a PC on every desk and in every home. He's only recently seen that the PC box isn't enough. Networking and the Internet change everything about computing. The Network is now the computer.

The biggest change in computing during the 1990s has been the huge expansion of computer networks (local and regional) and the Internet as a whole. Many offices at universities, law firms, government headquarters, and corporations are linked together via LANs and then linked from the LAN to the Internet. Programs and data files are now stored on central servers and shared by dozens, hundreds, even thousands of users. Plus, we now use our computers to communicate with our friends, colleagues, and business associates around the world. We're no longer limited by what can fit in our computer box or what this box can do on its own.

Some computer companies are now developing a basic Internet access computer for under $500; in other words, a computer that is nothing but Net. Other companies are looking at the market for a hybrid TV/Internet monitor that can be hooked up to a cable connection for both TV and Internet access. Most people will continue to use their computers for running programs on their hard drives as well as for accessing the Net and Web, but the transition from Box to Net is a major paradigm shift, both for hardware/software configurations and for users. This shift will continue through the late 1990s as the Web goes into its second generation with the ability to deliver programming along with data content.

The Web isn't just something "out there." Our computers become nodes in a network, and computing becomes living in an info-environment. Think of your Internet connection as an unlimited virtual disk drive: all the files and information you need are distributed on servers across the Net and instantly accessible. The Network is your computer. We're out of the Box and into the Net.

2.2 Why the Web Works: The Cross-platform and Software-independent Multimedia System

The genius of Internet technology is the ability to make otherwise incompatible computer systems talk to each other and to make them communicate with nonproprietary open standards. Macs, Intel/Windows PCs, UNIX machines, Vaxes, and IBM mainframes consist of self-contained operating systems and internal hardware, but Internet protocols allow all these incompatible systems to speak a common language. Since the Net is about moving bits to and from networked computers as efficiently as possible, all the computers on the Net need a common way to move those bits regardless of their own hardware and software configurations.

The Web takes this Internet premise several steps further by creating a hardware- and software-independent environment for all digital media. In practical terms, this means that whether you're using a Mac or Windows PC, each running its own version of Netscape, you'll be able to request files from, say, a UNIX Web server on the other side of the world. Your Web software will then seamlessly and transparently bring you the files and display them, even though they came from a very different, and incompatible, kind of computer.

Web users, Web content developers, and Web software companies have a big investment in keeping the protocols and standards open and capable of working on any system. The Web works only if the bitstream of information and content do not depend on specific pieces of software or hardware. Over the past few years, various companies have developed proprietary software or network links, but these companies inevitably shift to using the open standards of IP and the Web.

2.3 HTTP: The Daemon in the Machine

The Web is a multimedia bit-transporting system, and the engine that drives the Web is a special protocol for moving files from servers to clients on the Internet. Web server software is known as HTTPD, or the Hypertext Transport Protocol Daemon. ("Daemon" is a UNIX term for a program that runs in the background on a computer system and provides a service when called on. Most Internet server programs are called daemons; they come to life when they're hit with a request over the Net. A bit of hacker humor.) Web server software was developed as a way to deliver files in hypertext (HTML) format. When you see a URL with the **http://** prefix, you know that this points to a file on a Web server, an HTTP server. It's the interactivity between your client program and all the worldwide Web servers that makes the Web work. The Web allows for almost infinite expansion of content and programming with the Internet client–server architecture.

2.4 Using a Web Address: The URL

The Web works by requiring each file to have a unique "address," a unique name and place on a Web server. It's not enough to have the IP address of a server that has a file—there must be a way of pointing to or locating a file in a specific place on the server. This unique file address is called a Uniform Resource Locator (URL). A URL (pronounced U-R-L, not "earl") is a combination of the resource type or protocol, an Internet host name or server name, a directory path on the server, and a file name in a certain directory. A URL, therefore, points to a file at a particular location on a server on the Web. It's the location in Webspace that your Web client program needs to know to send out a file request.

In its basic or abstract form, a URL looks like this: *protocol://servername.domain/directory-path/filename*. Here are some examples:

http://home.netscape.com/index.html
gopher://ftp.std.com/11/obi/book/Emily.Bronte

ftp://ftp.ncsa.uiuc.edu/Mosaic/Windows/Win95/ mosaic20.exe

In these examples, we find the protocol, the server name and domain name, the directory path, and the file name. In the notation used on the Web, the protocol or resource type is followed by a colon and two forward slashes ("://").

These are the main protocol resource types that you will see in Web URLs:

http://	Hypertext Transport Protocol (the central web-specific protocol)
ftp://	File Transfer Protocol (link to a file on an FTP server)
gopher://	Gopher protocol (link to a file on a Gopher server)
telnet://	Telnet (remote login); starts up a telnet client and makes a remote telnet connection
news:	Access a file from or go to a Usenet newsgroup
mailto:	Send Internet email to the address defined in the link

Note: the **news:** and the **mailto:** resource types do not contain the closing slashes.

A URL is thus a unique address: there can be only one file with that name at that location on that server. The Web as a client–server system depends on the reliability of the URL: the server must be up and running and the file must be at the precise location pointed to in the URL for your client software to be able to fetch it for you.

Sometimes after you click on a hotlink, you'll get an error message telling you that the file or server (host) in the URL doesn't exist. This can mean "linkrot" has set in (the person maintaining the files moved or deleted these from the server) or that the server itself is down or has been taken off the Net for some reason. (Obviously, the Web works only if people maintain their files and keep their servers connected properly!) It may also mean that there is a typographical error somewhere in the URL. Remember that directory and file names are "case sensitive," that is, upper- and lower-case characters are treated as distinct computer characters in URLs. If you get an error message, check the case of all letters in directory and file names first.

You will find some URLs that do not have a file name indicated after the final slash; for example:

gopher://marvel.loc.gov/
http://www.georgetown.edu/grad/CCT/

The gopher server (for the Library of Congress) points to an index page of the top-level directory of the Library of Congress system. Accessing this URL brings you the top-level menu of this gopher server. On a Web server, a file name can be omitted if the URL points to the default file in the directory (normally named **index.html**). The home page for an organization or a starting page for any set of Web files can be set up this way so that Web users have a handier and shorter URL. For example, using **http://home.netscape.com/** (which actually points to a default file with the name **index.html** at the top level of the Web server directory) is handier than **http://home.netscape.com/index.html** (which is the full but longer URL). The longer the URL, the more potential for mistakes.

Most of the time you won't need to know the URL because it's provided in the hypertext link in a Web file that you are viewing. If you move your cursor over the highlighted text or a hot image, your Web client will display the URL for that link (in *Netscape Navigator*, the URL for a hotlink is displayed in the status line at the bottom of the program window). When you find a URL listed somewhere else—in an email message, an advertisement, a published article—you can always type it in on the location line in your Web client software.

2.5 The Web's Backward Compatibility: The Internet and the Web

A key feature of the Web for the user is its "backward" compatibility with earlier and existing Internet protocols and utilities. Everything that an ordinary user needs to do on the Internet can be done with good Web software like Netscape. Netscape is really a whole front-end or complete interface to the Internet, from email to Web hypermedia. For this reason, the term "Web" can be used for the whole array of protocols, Internet resources, and Internetworking tools accessible through Web client interface software.

Client software used for the Web incorporates the earlier file protocols developed for the Internet, but it's a good idea to

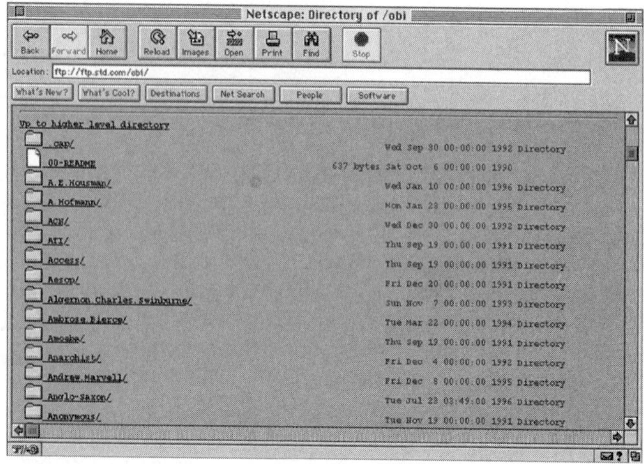

An FTP file as displayed in Netscape.

know what the other protocols are, since they are still widely used and often provide efficient ways of delivering information. You will often encounter links in Web files that use FTP, Gopher, and Telnet or point to Usenet Newsgroups and articles.

FTP

(URL Resource Type: ftp://)
FTP was initially done in text-only mode, using a set of commands typed at a command line. It got the job done, but you had to view or display the file transferred with another program as a second step. (The command-line language isn't too complicated, but it's not user friendly, especially in a time of point-and-click graphical interfaces.) Now files can be delivered from FTP servers and displayed in one step with Web client software.

FTP is still an efficient protocol for delivering digital media and software. You will often find image, video, sound, and software files hosted on FTP servers. A link to a file on an FTP server will be reflected in the URL that displays on the bottom status line of the Netscape window when you move the mouse over a hyperlink. When you click on the link, Netscape fetches and

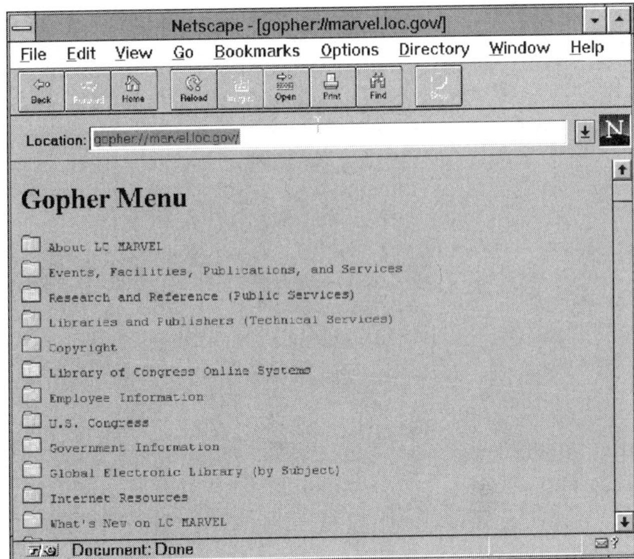

A Gopher directory or menu as displayed in Netscape.

displays the file (if it is in a medium supported by Netscape) and the **ftp://** will appear in the URL on the **Location** line.

You can also use Netscape to download software and other binary nondisplaying files from an FTP server to your computer. When you click on a link to this kind of file, Netscape will prompt you for the directory location and file name you want to download.

Gopher

(URL Resource Type: gopher://)

Gopher was a convenient way to arrange and navigate Net files before the Web and hypertext. Its limitations, of course, are the hierarchical menu structure and the closed or flat file format of plain-text files. A text file on a Gopher server is a dead end, not linkable to anything else.

Like FTP, Gopher servers are still commonly used for delivering a variety of media, and the URL with **gopher://** will display in Netscape when you have accessed a file from this type of server. And like FTP file transfers, Netscape will prompt you

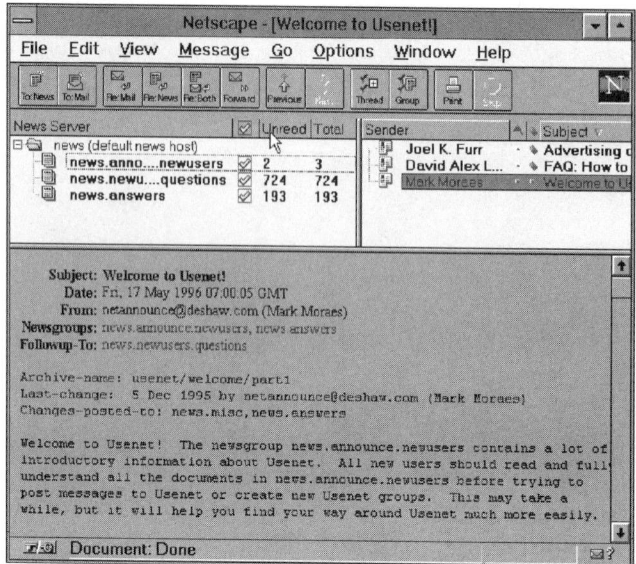

***Netscape Navigator*'s Usenet Newsreader window.**

for what to do with nondisplayable file types like software files or media that your client is not configured to display.

Usenet News: Newsreader Built into the Web Client Software

(URL Resource Type: news:)

Links to Usenet Newsgroups are passed on to Netscape's built-in newsreader program. A value-added feature of Netscape's newsreader is that URLs cited in news postings appear as hot-links that you can click on. The requested file is then displayed by Netscape in one step.

Before a newsreader program was integrated into Web client software, Usenet discussion group participants had to use a separate program to read and post messages. With Netscape, you can access a Usenet Newsgroup from a hyperlink (with a **news:*newsgroupname*** URL), or simply click on **Window | Netscape News** on the top menu bar. Either way, Netscape will launch a newsreader window, connect to the news server on

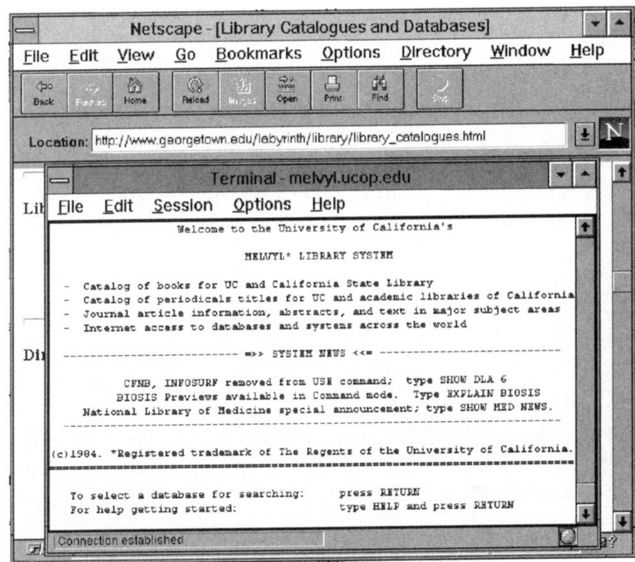

A telnet window for a telnet login (as a Netscape helper app).

your network, and display the message file or your subscribed newsgroups.

Telnet

(URL Resource Type: telnet://)
Many people use their direct Internet connection to telnet to email accounts on other systems or to connect to publicly accessible computers like library and government database systems. But a telnet link can't be established through a Web client in the same way that the client fetches files from FTP, Gopher, and Web servers. Telnet isn't a file transfer protocol but a remote operations protocol. It allows us to run programs like database software or email on another Internet computer. For this reason, a telnet client "helper application" needs to be configured for your Web client. (In Netscape, for example, you choose **Options** | **General Preferences** | **Apps** to install a telnet client to work within Netscape.) Most Internet providers supply their customers with a telnet program, and many freeware and shareware telnet programs are available for downloading on the Net.

The telnet interface is ordinarily in text-mode only (in a text-mode terminal emulation), and the software usable via a remote telnet session is ordinarily executed through commands on a system command line or through a simple menu display. The downside of telnet is that you are running software on the remote system and your computer becomes a terminal for it, thus subject to the limitations or features of the software on the remote system.

2.6 Web Interface Software: The Web Browser or Client Program

The Web gained great popularity in 1993 to 1995 because of the wide use of the graphical Web client programs *Mosaic* and *Netscape Navigator*, which share a common history of development. The original *Mosaic* was developed at the National Center for Supercomputer Applications (NCSA), at the University of Illinois, by a team led by Marc Andreesen. (The idea for the program began as his thesis project. Rumor has it that he passed.) Andreesen was hired by Netscape Communications, where he leads the team that developes the *Netscape Navigator* client, also known as *Mozilla* on the Web. (The name is hacker humor: it's a hybrid of "Mosaic" and "Godzilla," since the program is a "killer app.") Now over 80% of all Web users view the Web through one of the programs written by Andreesen and his team. NCSA Mosaic is still being developed at the University of Illinois by a new team of programmers, and there are several *Mosaic* clones and look-alikes on the market today.

The Web can be viewed from either a graphical interface (Windows, Mac, UNIX X-Windows) or text-only interface (such as VT–100 terminal emulation). The most popular graphical client programs as of 1996 are *Netscape Navigator* (over 70% of Web users), NCSA *Mosaic* (around 10% of users), and Microsoft's *Internet Explorer* (around 6% of users). For users accessing the Web in VT–100 text-only mode, *Lynx* is the most widely used text-only Web client (around 5% of users).[1] Now dozens

1. Stats on Web client usage can be found at The Browser Watch pages (**http://browserwatch.iworld.com/**), Interse's Web Trends (**http://www.interse.com/webtrends/**), and the client stats for requests from Yahoo's Random Links (**http://www.cen.uiuc.edu/~ejk/bryl.html**), as of January 1996. Dynamic client request stats are kept at the University of Illinois at Champaign-Urbana for all engineering workstations (**http://www.cen.uiuc.edu/bstats/latest.html**).

of Web client programs have been developed, though many are really of very poor quality and fail to come up to the standards of Netscape or NCSA Mosaic.

NOTE: *The Web software running on your local computer is commonly called a Web "browser," an unfortunate term now that the Web is really an interactive, multimedia system. To be consistent with Net terminology, these programs should be called "clients," since they interact with Web servers on the Net's client–server model.*

2.7 Hypertext and Hypermedia

The Web is a global, networked, hypertext system. Hypertext is electronic text freed from the constraints of texts as self-contained physical objects. Hypertext documents are interlinked, and the links among documents are marked by highlighted (or color-coded) words, phrases, or icons. The "hyper" in hypertext means going beyond and traversing the ordinary boundaries of texts as fixed, independent units. Hypertexts allow us to expose the interconnections among ideas and enable a whole new kind of authoring based on building multiple relationships among texts. A hypertext document is thus both text to be read and a map of other possible connections or associations beyond itself. Hypertext allows for unlimited connections among texts and within texts.

Hypermedia is a combination of hypertext and multimedia. Hypermedia likewise does not duplicate the constraints of conventional images, audio, and video in their isolated forms but allows for the linking of multiple media in an integrated form of presentation. The Web is actually a multimedia and hypermedia system: Digital media of any kind can be delivered to a user's computer and displayed in an integrated way through Web client software and other programs designed to play and display Web-delivered multimedia content.

Some hypertexts and hypermedia packages are self-contained databases that run on one computer or a local network, but the Web is a worldwide hypermedia system in which the linkable documents are distributed on computers all over the world. We can call the Web "hyperinteractive," which in our context combines "hypertext/hypermedia" and "interactive." The Web is designed for user-based interactivity and allows the linking of multiple documents and media in one interface.

A Brief History of Hypertext

Hypertext as a conceptual model for text and information linking has been around at least since 1945, the year Vannevar Bush published his famous article on the Memex machine. Bush is often credited with inventing the idea of a machine-based, indexed library, based on associational links. He called the machine that would perform these associations a "memex," and a memex user would build an indexed trail of associated terms, facts, and ideas to form a knowledge base on a subject. In short, a hypertext trail. But Bush imagined all this as a microfilm database.

In 1965, Ted Nelson coined the term "hypertext" for a kind of text based on unlimited associative links with other texts, and in 1985 he imagined the possibility of a vast global hypertext database which he called "Xanadu." Steps toward realizing this idea were undertaken at Brown University in 1985 with the Intermedia Project. Many people first came to appreciate the power of hypertext in Apple's *HyperCard* authoring software, a kind of hypermedia erector set, introduced in 1987.

But the idea of a worldwide hypertext system using the Internet was first proposed by Tim Berners-Lee in 1989. The World Wide Web was launched by Berners-Lee soon afterward at CERN, but in its initial stage, the Web was a hypertext rather than a full hypermedia system. In June 1993, *Mosaic* became available, and the graphical interface expanded the capabilities of the Web for multimedia. The rest, as we say, is history.

USER NOTE
HTML CONCEPTS

HTML is kind of a hybrid markup language since it defines the *logical structure* of a document (headings, titles, and paragraphs, for example) and also supplies *formatting and display features* (image placement, text alignment, and color background, for example). But its *power* for the Internet's client–server system is the method for *hyperlinking* files together to form a *multimedia web*, so that any Web file can be linked to any other on any Web server.

There are now several versions, or levels, of HTML. HTML 2.0 is the accepted standard, but Netscape Extensions to 2.0, though not universally accepted, have become a de facto standard as a result of their wide use. Currently the standards for HTML version 3.0 are still under discussion. The *markup features continue to evolve* as new standards emerge from creative applications of Web technology. HTML has limitations, but it is widely accepted as a versatile markup scheme for networked document delivery and publishing.

2.8 HTML (Hypertext Markup Language): How Web Files Are Encoded

HTML is a set of tags or codes written into a text file that provide instructions for your Web client. HTML as a "markup language" is based on international standards established for SGML (Standard Generalized Markup Language), and HTML is sometimes called a subset of SGML. HTML files are actually just plain text or ASCII files containing HTML tags. The tags are known as "meta" elements in a file because they are not displayed as part of the content of a file but function as instructions that tell your client what to do with what's in the file. HTML tags provide instructions for formatting a file for the screen, inserting images, and creating the hypertext links that bring you other files from the Web. Web files in HTML have the file extension **.html** or **.htm** and all Web clients know how to interpret these files.

HTML is an integral part of the whole Web concept in that it is not hardware- or software-dependent. Have you ever had trouble exchanging files with someone using a different computer platform or a different program? Most computing today still butts up against the brick wall of incompatible file types or hardware types. Not so with the Web. The genius of HTML and SGML is that they are machine-independent ways of encoding electronic text files so that any computer can use them.

If you've ever needed to work with text-formatting codes in your word processor, like *WordPerfect*, for example, you are familiar with the idea of codes embedded in a file that do not display on the screen but rather tell your software *how* to display the file. Many HTML tags work the same way but are much easier to learn, since they are written as plain text and can be composed or edited with any text editor.

2.9 How to Read HTML Files

HTML tags are enclosed by angle brackets ("⟨" and "⟩"). Any markup put in angle brackets will not be displayed as text in a Web client program. Tags that define a structural element or formatting feature in the file, like italics or a heading, have a beginning and ending element, like an on and off switch. The ending tag is marked by a forward slash ("/"). For example, here's a simple HTML file containing one "heading" element and a few formatting tags.

```
⟨html⟩
⟨body⟩
⟨h1⟩HTML Demo Page for Web Works⟨/h1⟩
Greetings! Hope you are enjoying ⟨i⟩Web Works⟨/i⟩. You'll
notice that when this paragraph is displayed in a
⟨b⟩Netscape⟨/b⟩ window the markup tags do not appear,
and the text of the paragraph wraps line by line to fit the
size of the window.
⟨p⟩
HTML files are just plain text files like this stored on Web
servers. As you can see, they're fairly straightforward. All
the markup in the angle brackets is interpreted but not
displayed by the Web client.
⟨p⟩
⟨/body⟩
⟨/html⟩
```

Basic formatting tags appear then as "⟨*tag*⟩ . . . ⟨/*tag*⟩," where *tag* is whatever is being defined. Note that HTML markup, unlike Web directory and file names, is not case-sensitive: you can use upper- or lower-case characters when writing the tags since Web client programs read them either way (i.e., H1 is the same as h1). Here's how the file above looks in Netscape:

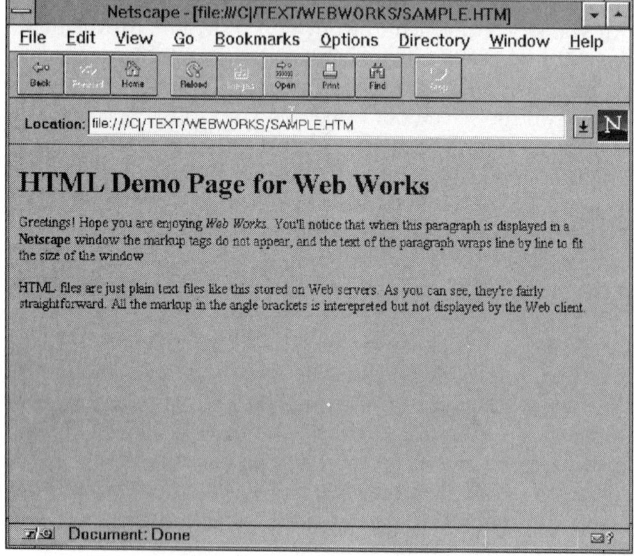

Sample HTML file as displayed in Netscape.

Strictly speaking, there are two essential tags that define an HTML file—the ⟨html⟩ . . . ⟨/html⟩ and ⟨body⟩ . . . ⟨/body⟩ tags. The beginning and ending ⟨html⟩ tags are required; they define the whole document as an HTML file. The ⟨body⟩ tags tell the client program where the main body of the document begins and ends. The heading tags, ⟨H1⟩ . . . ⟨/H1⟩, define the first or major heading in a document, and the text marked with these tags will be displayed in large, bold type, and separated from the text that follows. (Heading elements range from H1 to H6, indicating logical relationships in a text and corresponding size of bold text that will be displayed.) As you may have guessed, ⟨i⟩ . . . ⟨/i⟩ and ⟨b⟩ . . . ⟨/b⟩ are tags for italics and boldfaced text, and ⟨p⟩ marks a paragraph break.

You can always view the source file with the HTML markup in Netscape by clicking on **View** in the top menu bar, then **View Document Source**. Studying the tags in a **View Source** window is a good way to learn how the markup works since you can view the HTML source file along with the way it displays in Netscape (see also Chapter 8).

2.10 Using Hypertext and Hyperlinks

Use of the Net and Web expanded quickly during the mid-1990s because graphical interface software greatly simplified the user's need to navigate all the widely-distributed information resources. The first Web browser software developed at CERN was a simple text-mode interface that worked with menus and commands. *Lynx*, another popular text-only client developed at the University of Kansas, used highlighted text and simple navigation with arrow keys and commands, many of which were modeled on the Gopher interface (also text only). But with graphical interface clients like *Mosaic* and *Netscape Navigator*, there are no commands to learn, and nothing to type in unless you insert a new URL in the **Location** box or use **File | Open Location** from the menu bar.

Hotlinks or hyperlinks can be highlighted words or text, icons and buttons, or sections of an image that have been encoded to provide links to other files. Graphical interface software also allows much fuller user interaction with the Web, including forms, multiple simultaneous windows (the "frames" feature of Netscape 2.0), and a whole new array of applications that can be run by interacting with the Web server (see also Chapter 7).

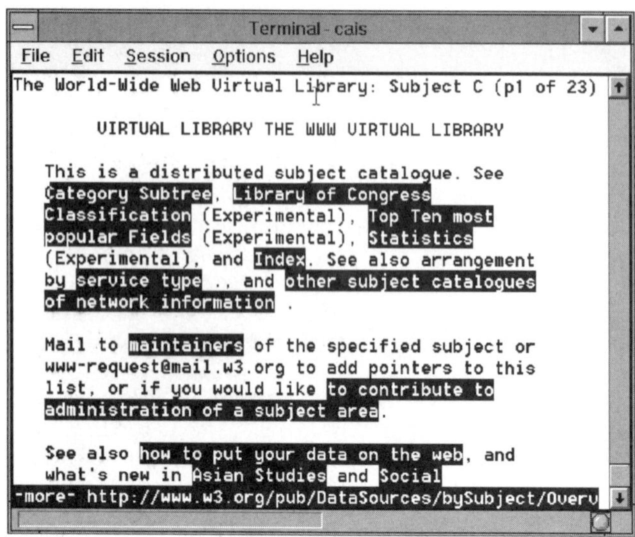

Web file viewed with *Lynx*, a text-only client.

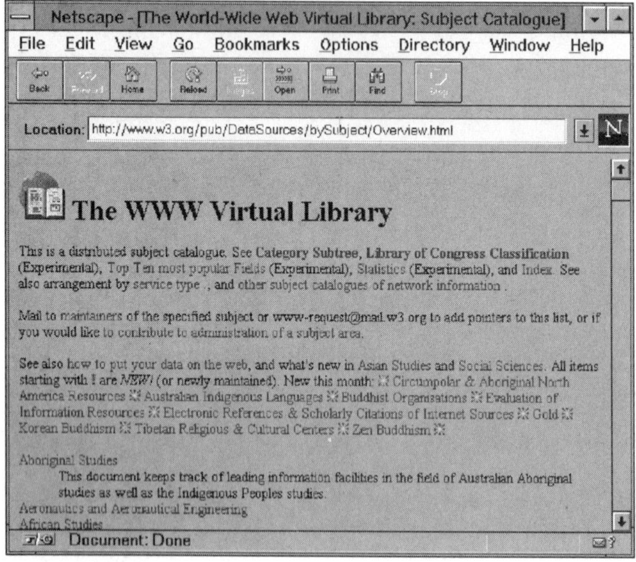

Same file viewed with *Netscape Navigator*.

2.11 What Happens When We Click on a Link: A Look behind the Scenes

It's important to have a sense of what's going on behind the scenes when we click on a hotlink in a Web file. Understanding the basic concepts of how your client program works and interacts with the Web will make it much easier to navigate the Web now, use new Web software as it is developed, and troubleshoot problems that may occur. (We'll continue to use *Netscape Navigator* as our reference client program and use a link to a Web server—an HTTP server—to illustrate what happens when we click on a link.) You can watch much of what's happening behind the scenes as it's being reported in the **status line** at the bottom of a Netscape window.

USER NOTE
WHEN YOU CLICK ON A HOTLINK . . .

1. Netscape knows the IP address of the local computer you're using because the networking software for connecting to the Internet (the TCP/IP software) is already loaded on your system. Netscape uses this address for all interactions with the Internet.

2. Netscape reads the server named in the URL encoded in the hotlink and sends a request to look up the domain name, to a Name Server (the Domain Name System server used in your network region).

3. The Name Server sends back the IP address of the Web server that Netscape requested, and then Netscape sends out a file transfer request over the Internet to the IP address of the server.

4. The HTTP server recognizes the request, checks to see if the file named in the URL exists and can be sent, and then sends the file over the Internet to your IP address. The Web server can send the file if and only if it exists at the directory path location specified in the URL and if the file is available to the public (has been given world access permission on the server). If the file named in the URL doesn't exist or hasn't been set to "world readable" on the server, you'll get an error message back from the server.

5. Finally, Netscape reads the incoming file and displays it on your screen. (If Netscape encounters a file type that it can't handle internally, it launches or prompts you for another application with which to play or display the file.)

These steps are followed from your computer to the Web server when all the layers of client–server interaction work properly. But what happens when one or more of the steps don't work?

2.12 Basic Web Troubleshooting

We've seen how the Internet and World Wide Web are complex, shared, networking systems with a simplified front-end

USER NOTE
TROUBLESHOOTING LIST

Apparent Problem	What It May Mean	What to Do
Netscape won't boot or run.	TCP/IP software (Winsock or Mac TCP/IP) is not loaded or configured; Netscape can't find TCP/IP files.	Check to see if system is configured for TCP/IP. For *Win* 3.1 systems, check if the directory for TCP/IP software is listed in directory path of your autoexec.bat file. For Macs, be sure MacTCP is installed (check under **Control Panels**). Get user support if possible.
"Netscape is unable to locate the server (Failed DNS Lookup)" error message appears.	Netscape sent out a Name Server lookup request, but (1) couldn't find the Name Server on your network, (2) your network connection may be down, or (3) the Name Server couldn't match the name to an IP address.	Retry: click on the link again or retype the URL. (1 and 2) If a retry fails, check to see if other network functions work (telnet, for example). (3) The server named in the URL isn't in the DNS database; it could be mistyped, renamed, off the Net, or a faulty name.

(the client program). Although the client program makes the work of the network seem transparent, we need specific information to understand how things can go wrong (or seem to at first). As you use the Web, you'll encounter various error messages from network servers, failed searches, stalled or hung up file requests after you click on a link, and slow or delayed incoming files. The good news: most of the time, the things that can go wrong have nothing to do with you, and you can't break anything. Most of the problems that ordinary users encounter

Apparent Problem	What It May Mean	What to Do
"Error: File Not Found" or similar message appears after clicking on a link or inserting a URL in the **Location** line.	File does not exist at the location specified in the URL. File name may be mistyped or misspelled. Linkrot may have set in (the person owning the file moved, removed, or renamed it).	If you have typed in a URL, make sure everything is spelled correctly (including upper- and lower-case characters). If linkrot is the cause, you may be able to navigate around in related directories to see if the file has been moved or renamed (delete the file name and/or last directory in the URL and hit **Return/ Enter**). If a file can't be located where a URL points to, there's nothing a user can do; skip it and move on. If it's important, email the file owner or Webmaster.
File or image stalls or stops when loading.	Network traffic may be slowing transmission from server. Server may have long queue of requests. File may have been corrupted in transit.	Click on the **Stop** button. Then click on **Reload**. A new server request often clears up the problem.

are easily identifiable and (usually) fixable. The bad news: there are many layers to Internetworking, and many features to the software you use on your end, and it's sometimes difficult to identify a problem and fix it. Here's where background on how the Web works becomes important for all users.

So we're back to the user orientation of the Web for problem solving. If things don't work the way you hoped or expected, try not to get too frustrated and don't worry about whose fault it is, even when you're in the middle of a task and need the Web to deliver quickly. This section provides strategies for figuring out where the problem might be: Is it on your end (your computer, the client program, your access to the network) or

USER NOTE
TROUBLESHOOTING LIST *(continued)*

Apparent Problem	What It May Mean	What to Do
Images take too long to load.	Local bandwidth and your Net connection may not be up to delivering large files like images and video quickly.	If you are using a set of files where text information is more important, turn off the **Autoload Images** feature in the **Options** menu. When you reload the file it will come more quickly as text alone.
Everything seems slow.	Possible contributors: low bandwidth on your network, network traffic jams, overworked server, not enough RAM on your system.	Bandwidth is always a problem. If you are using an Internet Service Provider (ISP), ask them about the problem. Switch to an ISP with faster Net access. Check to see if you have enough RAM on your computer for efficient Netscape and network use (see Chapter 3).

on the other end (on the server side or somewhere along the Internet)?

Without getting too technical, we can think in terms of four kinds of problems, some of which permit user solutions: Is the problem (1) on the client side (your system and software), (2) on the server side (remote system), (3) at the level of your Internet access and local network, or (4) at the level of the Internet system (traffic jams, transfer errors, long queues at busy servers)? The "Troubleshooting List" notes common problems and suggestions for fixing them.

We've been using *Netscape Navigator* as our reference Web client for many reasons, and one good one is Netscape's online *Handbook*, which includes answers to basic questions and tutorials on using Netscape's features. (To use the online handbook, click on **Help** at the top menu bar, and then choose **Handbook**.) If you have questions about using any of Netscape's features, go to the *Handbook* first, since it will always have the most up-to-date advice.

BACKGROUND INFORMATION

Site	URL
BrowserWatch for Web Software	**http://browserwatch.iworld.com/**
Vannevar Bush on Memex ("As We May Think")	**http://www.isg.sfu.ca/~duchier/misc/vbush/**
Hypertext terms	**http://www.w3.org/hypertext/WWW/Terms.html**
Hypermedia Timeline	**http://www.eit.com/web/www.guide/guide.14.html**
Guides to the Web and HTML	**http://www.georgetown.edu/labyrinth/general/general.html**

3
Getting Connected

Internet access is rapidly becoming another utility industry like cable TV and telephone service. With the Telecommunications Reform Act of 1996, many companies in these industries will be combining services, and we may soon be able to get cable TV, telephone, and Internet access all from one company. (Whether this will be a good or bad thing remains to be seen.) The downside for individual users, at least in the short term, is that Internet access is not standardized: getting connected is not quite as easy as buying a phone from a discount appliance store and plugging it into a phone jack. But with a little background on what's needed, you'll be able to set up your own connection.

To get your computer connected to the Net you need

- The right equipment at your end.
- The right software for making the Internet connection.
- The right telecommunications link that will make your computer networthy, usually supplied by an Internet Service Provider (ISP).

If you don't have Internet access already, or want t[…]now what to ask for to get connected at your office or hom[…] you'll need to know (1) the kinds of Internet connections […]at are available, (2) the hardware needed, (3) the software […]eded, and (4) the kinds of services provided.

3.1 Kinds of Internet Co[…]ections

There are really only two k[…] connections to the Internet, direct and indirect, and […]eed and user control, the direct connection is prefer[…]he telecommunications industry expands in the era […]e Telecom Reform Act of 1996, there will be several […] options and levels of connectivity f[…]

Internet access at home and work. Here is a description of the basic types of Internet access that most users will continue to find available.

A Direct Connection

With a direct connection, your computer is assigned an IP address and interacts directly with other Internet computers. Examples of direct Internet connections are a LAN connection to the Net or a single computer using a modem connection to an Internet server (SLIP/PPP) with a graphical interface.

With a direct Internet connection, your own computer is assigned an IP address, allowing your client software to interact directly with all the servers on the Net. This is what is meant by a "direct" connection: with an IP address, you are on the Net.

If you are using the Net from a university or corporate computer, you are probably connected to the Net via a LAN. If you have your Net connection already established for you via a LAN, you won't need to be concerned about the details for connectivity and configuring software outlined here. If you're also interested in an Internet connection at home or office through a single telephone line, read on.

An Indirect Connection

An indirect or brokered connection via an online service like CompuServe, Prodigy, or America Online does not assign your computer an IP address but provides Internet connectivity through another computer running proprietary networking software; for example, the Web browser in AOL or CompuServe's software interface.

Indirect Internet connections through an online service provide a buffer between the user and the technology. Your computer is not assigned an IP address, and you are not on the Net. These are "brokered" connections because you have to use a proprietary non-IP connection to the online service's computer to get your Net and W[illegible] [illegible]nnection.

NOTE: *There is another way [illegible] the Internet through a modem connection, the "shell" accoun[illegible] [illegible] Internet server, but it is not a direct connection and the access t[illegible] [illegible] is text-only mode. ("Shell" is a UNIX term for the level in the [illegible] system at which a user types in commands on a command li[illegible] [illegible]ystem prompt.) Many*

ISPs provide this type of dial-up connection to an account on a server connected to the Internet. This service does not assign your computer an IP address and you must use the client software on the provider's computer for performing Net and Web functions like telnet, FTP, and Web access. A shell account is useful for email, however, and many ISPs provide a shell account for their SLIP/PPP customers for this purpose.

Some people have found using the Web browsers provided by online services an easy way to get started with learning the Web. You should be aware, however, that the commercial service acts as a go-between or broker for Internet access and content, content which is free to direct Internet users. If what you want is the Web and not the specially developed content or services of an AOL or CompuServe, then you should connect with a direct Internet provider. (AOL, CompuServe, and AT&T now provide true Internet services also. For ISPs, see "Questions for Internet Service Providers," on pages 50–51.) Direct Internet access is usually cheaper and faster than getting your connection through a proprietary online service. This book can't provide information for the commercial online services. The information in this chapter is for people wanting to get a direct connection with an ISP.

3.2 Internet Connection Requirements

If you have a LAN connection at a lab or office, you won't need to be concerned with the first two requirements here. For a direct Internet connection that allows you to run client programs like Netscape from home or from a single phone line anywhere, you need a computer with the TCP/IP software, a modem to connect your computer to the Internet server, and an Internet connection through an Internet Service Provider.

1. A Computer That Can Run the Software for Your TCP/IP Connection

The major platforms for Internetworking are Intel/Windows PCs, Macs, and Unix systems. The software that you'll need for making your computer Internet-worthy is free or inexpensive, either public domain or shareware programs (like *Trumpet Winsock*) or software already provided with your operating system (as in Windows 95 and Macintosh System 7.5).

The TCP/IP software needed on your end is usually referred

to as the "TCP/IP stack," meaning the layers of networking instructions required to make an Internet connection. For PCs, Windows 3.1/3.11 requires a properly configured Winsock (short for "Windows sockets") TCP/IP stack. This is supplied by a file named winsock.dll and related files.

A shareware TCP/IP Winsock program is *Trumpet Winsock,* available via FTP on many Internet sites and provided by most ISPs. This program includes a dialer (to allow your modem to dial in and link to an ISP's modems) and the winsock.dll file for making the Internet connection. A dialer and TCP/IP package is provided in *Netscape Navigator Personal* edition, which allows an easy setup of your modem type and the phone number of your ISP. The TCP/IP software is integrated with the operating system (OS) in Windows 95 and Macintosh System 7.5. (If you use a lower version of the Mac OS, you will need to install MacTCP.) Most Internet Service Providers supply the basic software and an automatic installation routine that will set up the software on your hard drive and configure the software to work with your modem (see section 3.5).

2. A Modem or Hardware Device That Links Your Computer to the Net

There are several kinds of devices that are used for specific kinds of network connections:

- A modem for connections over ordinary phone lines.
- A modem for an ISDN connection (high-speed dedicated line).
- A cable modem (for high-speed cable connections).
- An ethernet or other networking card for a LAN.

For home use, a 28.8 kilobits per second (kbps) modem is standard for an Internet connection over ordinary phone lines. Some areas now have faster connections via ISDN and cable. Check with your phone or cable company to see if this service is available.

ISDN (an acronym for the unwieldy Integrated Services Digital Network) and cable Internet service are only just becoming widely available. ISDN technology allows concurrent transmission of voice, video, and digital data, and you can actually use an ISDN line for a voice phone call simultaneously with your Internet connection, though the speed for your digital data transfer will decrease. ISDN requires a special modem designed for this data transmission method. ISDN data speeds are much higher than conventional modems, available at 64 and 128 kbps.

Cable companies like TCI and Jones Intercable are now offering digital data links and Internet connections through cable lines, and this technology requires a cable modem for your computer. Data transmission speeds with cable are very impressive, and when the technology is refined and becomes widely available, there will be a great demand for this kind of Internet connectivity.

An ethernet card is the usual way to connect a computer to a LAN. If your office has LAN connectivity available, you probably already have the support needed to connect your computer.

3. An Internet Connection Provider

There are now many regional, national, and even international Internet Service Providers. Here's how an ISP connects you to the Net. For connections across ordinary phone lines, an ISP provides the TCP/IP connection for your computer through a dedicated server linked directly to the Net. The service provider's computer is connected to a bank of modems that you connect to with your modem. When you dial in to the ISP's modems, your computer is assigned an IP address using SLIP (Serial Line Internet Protocol) or PPP (Point-to-Point Protocol) a methods for providing IP connections over ordinary phone lines.

If you use a LAN at an office or university, the necessary TCP/IP connectivity has most likely already been set up. Web and Net client software is so popular now that you should find it on your system. If not, ask your LAN administrator or support person to install World Wide Web client programs and the required helper applications needed for using special kinds of files (for example, video and special graphics formats).

3.3 Hardware Recommendations for Best Results

For modems, there is a standard rule (forgetting price for the moment): buy the highest-speed modem available that conforms to all the current industry standards for data transmis-

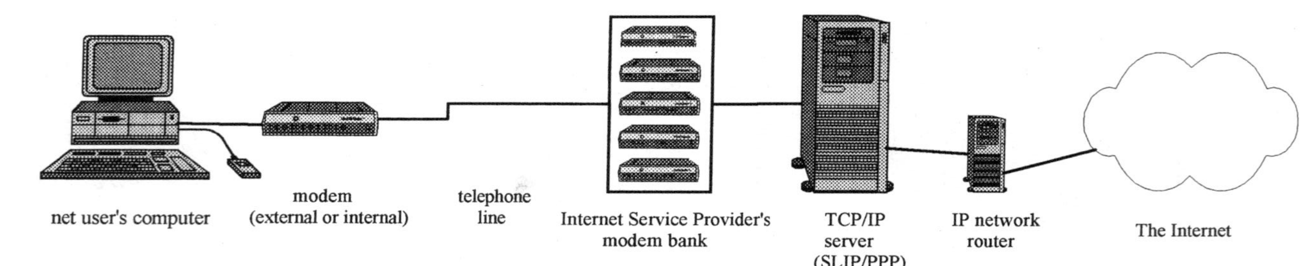

Connecting to the Internet with an Internet Service Provider.

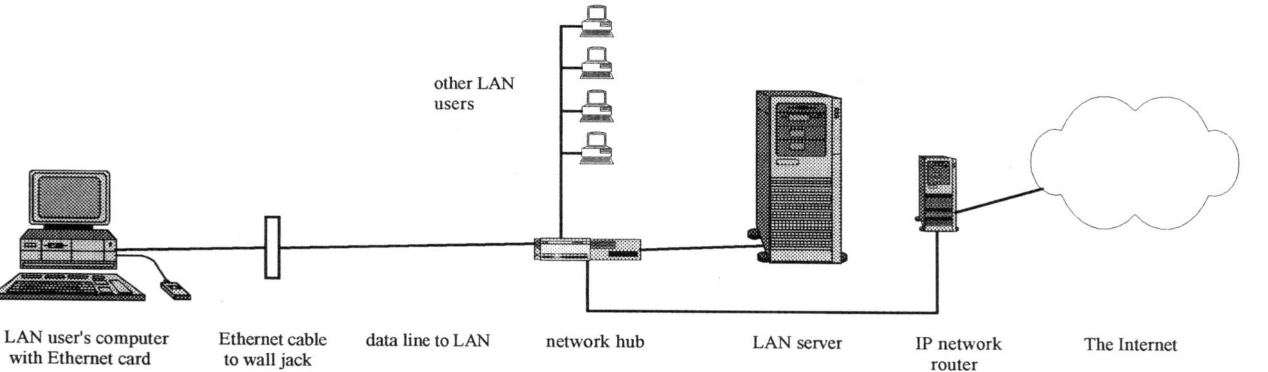

Connecting to the Internet via Ethernet and LAN.

sion. Speed for modems, and just about any data connection, is measured in thousands of bits per second (kbps, kilobits per second, also known as baud rate). An industry standard has been established for 14.4 and 28.8 kbps (called "14, 4" and "28, 8") modems using data compression and error correction protocols. (The industry standard now is 28.8 kbps modems using a form of data compression called V.34.) Because of the kind of data compression used in 28.8 modems, the actual speed of the data transmission, known as "throughput," can be higher than the modem's nominal speed. Depending on your connection at the other end, that is, the speed of your Net provider's modems and Internet connection, the speed of a 28.8 modem can sometimes be two to four times greater than 28.8 kbps.

If you're about to buy a modem, consider modems by US Robotics, a leader in reliable modem technology. There are many other good standard brands, but buying an off-brand because it's a little cheaper buys you more problems if something doesn't work. The price of modems fluctuates with the introduction of higher speed capability and new data protocols, but 28.8 modems are now very affordable.

For the home and office user, Windows PCs (Intel microprocessor computers running Microsoft Windows) are more easily networkable, but there is also TCP/IP software for Macintosh systems. Here are some recommendations.

3.4 What Is an Internet Service Provider?

An Internet Access Provider (IAP) or Internet Service Provider (ISP) provides the connection to the Internet. Depending on

USER NOTE
SYSTEM REQUIREMENTS FOR WINDOWS PCs

Adequate	Better
Any 386 or 486 system	486–66 through Pentium systems
8 MB RAM	16 MB RAM
14.4 kbps modem	28.8 kbps modem
14-inch SVGA monitor	15-inch (or larger) SVGA monitor

the size and market of the company, an ISP can provide simple modem connections over ordinary phone lines or high-speed data connections using dedicated data lines. Big national companies like PSI, UUNet, and Netcom offer a wide range of connectivity types, data speeds, and rates. Many local companies do the same.

Think of ISPs as TCP/IP utility companies that connect you to the Net through their own systems and routers. You need a phone company to connect your phone to the rest of the world's phone system, and you need an ISP to give your computer the IP connection that will allow it to interact with other computers on the Net.

Internet access is now big business, but since this utility industry is new and not yet standardized, we customers need some solid information to make smart choices and to get good service. Many cities in North America are seeing Internet service price wars, and many local ISPs are competing to subscribe users at very low prices. Ten to fifteen dollars per month, with unlimited or many hours of use per day, is now offered in some cities. You should not have to pay more than $25 to $30 per month for Internet access from a national ISP.

3.5 Finding a Good Internet Service Provider

Your Internet Service Provider should be able to answer the questions on pp. 50–51 to your satisfaction. Some companies provide information for some of these basic questions on their Websites.

USER NOTE
SYSTEM REQUIREMENTS FOR MACINTOSH

Adequate	Better
68030 system	68040 through Power PC
8 MB RAM	16 MB RAM
14.4 kbps modem	28.8 kbps modem
14-inch Color Plus Display	15-inch Multi-Scan Display

USER NOTE
QUESTIONS FOR INTERNET SERVICE PROVIDERS

Question	Comments
1. How do you handle user support? Do you have a toll-free customer support line? What are the hours?	Check to see if they have a dedicated phone line for user support and if you can call them over a generous time period throughout the day and times you use your computer (weekends? evenings?).
2. Is a call to your modems from my area code a local phone call?	Obviously a factor for cost to the user.
3. How long have you been in the Internet service business? How many user accounts do you have?	Many companies are new, but you should be able to get a sense of their track record. Find out how many user accounts they have.
4. How many modems do you have, and what is the ratio of modems to user accounts?	To prevent busy signals, the best ratio is no more than 10:1, customers to modems. All customers will never be logged in to the Internet server at once, so this is a good rule of thumb.
5. Are all of your modems 28.8 kbps?	Some ISPs may still be using slower modem connections. Count those out.
6. What is the speed of your server's connection to the Internet?	Accept nothing less than a T1 connection (a standard high-speed link), and some providers have T3 connections (one of the highest speeds available).

Question	Comments
7. How often have your computers been down in the past year? What is the average down time?	All servers go down occasionally, but they should never be down for long.
8. Do you provide the Internet (TCP/IP) software and a Web client (Netscape) with the account? Is the software free?	The ISP should provide all the necessary software and the setup routine for installing it. Most provide it free with the account.
9. What is your pricing schedule? Do you have a flat-rate unlimited use price plan? Is there a startup fee?	Many ISPs have competitive flat-rate accounts. This is the best account to get if you want to use the Web a lot and don't want to think about the meter running.
10. Do you provide access to a Web server for customers' personal pages? Is there an extra charge?	As you become familiar with the Web, you will quickly want to start putting up your own information on the Web. You'll need access to a Web server (an HTTP server) to do this.
11. Do you have Points of Presence (local dial-in points) in other cities?	This can be important if you want Net access while on the road. With a notebook computer and a modem card, you're Networthy wherever you go if your provider covers the areas you travel to.

A national provider is a good way to get Internet access if you want to be connected wherever you go. Below is a list of some national ISPs in the United States.

Pricing schedules may change with a provider's marketing strategies. Check *Internet World, PC Magazine,* the provider's Website, and the business section of major city newspapers for ISP ads and current prices.

USER NOTE
DIRECT ISPs WITH NATIONAL (U.S.) COVERAGE

Provider	Website
Concentric Network 800–939–4262	**http://www.cris.com**
GNN (owned by AOL) 800–819–6112	**http://www.gnn.com/gnn/join/index.html**
IDT 800–245–8000	**http://www.idt.net**
Netcom 800–353–6600	**http://www.netcom.com**
AT&T WorldNet 800–967–5363	**http://www.att.com/worldnet/wis/**
MCI InternetMCI 800-955-5210	**http://www.mci.com/resources/forhome/**
CompuServe SpryNet 800–777–9638	**http://www.sprynet.com**
MindSpring 404-815-0082	**http://www.mindspring.com**
Earthlink 818-296-2400	**http://www.earthlink.net**

The ISP business is growing, expanding, and changing very rapidly; the best place to find up-to-date information about ISPs is on the Web. That creates a catch–22 for new users looking for a provider: how do you get to information on the Web if you're not already connected? If you have Web access at work or can borrow a friend's computer, you can find other useful background information and search for a good ISP on the following Websites.

Price	Comments
Various plans: $19/month and $29/month based on prepayment	Good U.S. coverage. Network access sometimes slow.
$14.95/month for 20 hours; $1.95/additional hour	AOL dial-in numbers, 28.8 modems not in all areas.
$29/month for unlimited access.	Good price. Support needs work.
$19.95/month for 40 prime-time hours; $2/additional hour; unlimited off-peak and weekend access.	Good coverage of U.S. cities; 28.8 modem connectivity.
$19.95/month for unlimited access for AT&T customers; $24.95 month for non-AT&T customers.	New service by AT&T.
$19.95/month for unlimited local dial-in access.	MCI has been in the Internet business for several years.
$19.95/month for unlimited access; other price plans available.	An Internet service by CompuServe.
$19.95/month for unlimited access.	Fast-growing company; bought PSINet's dial-up service.
$19.95/month for unlimited access.	Fast-growing company.

INTERNET ACCESS

URL	Information
http://www.yahoo.com/Business_and_Economy/Companies/Internet_Services/Internet_Access_Providers/	Yahoo Index for Internet Access Providers
http://www.thelist.com/	Mecklermedia's List of ISPs (United States and worldwide)
http://www.netusa.net/ISP/	Useful ISP index by country; for the United States, by state and area code
http://www.celestin.com/pocia/index.html	Providers of Commercial Internet Access Directory
http://www.commerce.net/directories/products/isp/	CommerceNet's Directory of ISPs
http://www.charm.net/pip.html	Guides for individual PC Internet connectivity
news:alt.internet.services	Frank rants and raves about ISPs

NET AND WEB APPLICATIONS AND TOOLS

Application	Sites
Windows and Winsock software and applications (Stroud's Consummate Winsock Apps List)	**http://www.cwsapps.com/cwsa.html** Mirror sites **http://www.cwsapps.com/cwsapps.html** **http://www.caboose.com/cwsapps/cwsapps.html**
Best Quick-Start Internet apps for new Windows users	**http://www.cwsapps.com/casper.html**
Windows Net and Web Tools List (Ian Graham, University of Toronto)	**http://www.utirc.utoronto.ca/HTMLdocs/pc_tools.html**
Mac software and applications for the Web	**http://wwwhost.ots.utexas.edu/mac/internet.html** **http://www.utirc.utoronto.ca/HTMLdocs/mac_tools.html**

4
Using the Web for Research

The Web is a distributed system of information on servers all over the Internet. This makes the Web an excellent resource for all kinds of research and information hunting. We can use library catalogs and databases at research centers as well as the universe of files on Web servers hosted by information-producing organizations. But without a way to index, catalog, and search all the millions of files, the Web would be like a vast unsorted archive of documents and artifacts that none but a master archivist could use. Web technology has produced very fast searching and retrieval utilities known as "search engines," which allow us to find information on any topic. When the search results come in, the user can then evaluate them for relevance, quality, and reliability. Some Websites are devoted to cataloging and indexing information resources by category or general topic. This chapter introduces the tools for using library catalogs and databases, and for searching the entire Web for specific information.

There are thus different kinds of search strategies for finding the information we need. Sometimes we may want a larger context for research (like browsing the books on library shelves next to the specific book we are looking for), sometimes we want all there is on a general topic (a large list of everything available), sometimes we want information only on a very well defined topic, name, or title (a strictly defined search inquiry). We may also want to search the contents of a single file to check for occurrences of keywords, names, or special terms and the contexts in which they are used. To do a successful Web search, then, we need to match a search objective with the right tool.

The important thing to learn is how to find what we're looking for without wasting time. To achieve this, we need to know how to use the best search-and-discovery tools.

The Web allows searches for specific objectives:

- *Information in the broadest sense.* Any topic or subject.
- *Corporate and commercial information.* Companies and services on the Internet.
- *Software.* Public domain and shareware programs downloadable from the Net.
- *People.* Directories of individuals on the Net.
- *Groups and communities of people.* Discussion groups and lists, special-interest groups.

And tools designed for various search methods:

- **Search or browse** the contents of Web **catalogs and topical indices** that arrange information resources **by category**.

INFORMATION SITE 5

NET DIRECTORIES, CATALOGS, AND TOPICAL INDICES

Site	URL	Comments
Netscape's **Net Directory** list	**http://home.netscape.com/home/internet-directory.html** Or click on **Directory** | **Internet Directory**)	Excellent up-to-date index of major commercial Net subject directories. Good place to start to learn how to use them. General audience.
Library of Congress's Meta–Index	**http://lcweb.loc.gov/global/metaindex.html**	A useful index of all the Web indices. A good place to start as an orientation to using Web indices. General audience.
Yahoo	**http://www.yahoo.com/**	Large searchable index of Web information resources by category. Also allows searches of the index by subject. General and popular audience.
GNN Whole Internet Catalogue	**http://gnn.com/wic/wics/index.html**	Reliable catalog of the Net and Web. General audience.
InfoSeek Guide	**http://www.infoseek.com/**	Good index of Web resources with search engine. General audience.

- **Search** Web and Net files **by keyword(s) or phrases** with a search engine that performs a search **on millions of indexed Web files**.
- **Search** files on a **specific Website** or collection of resources.
- **Search** the contents of a **specific file** for **occurrences of keywords** or phrases.

4.1 Looking Things Up: Using Directories and Indices

Let's plug in an example. If you are just beginning to explore a particular topic on the Web—for example, environmental law—it's generally a good idea to start with an index or directory like those listed in "Information Site 5" (below) that or-

Site	URL	Comments
EINet Galaxy	**http://www.einet.net/galaxy.html**	Topical searchable catalog of Internet resources. General audience.
WWW Virtual Library	**http://www.w3.org/hypertext/DataSources/bySubject/Overview.html**	The largest subject catalog. Hosted by the W3 Consortium, the WWW VL is a distributed catalog, each main subject page maintained by a specialist in the subject area. General and research-oriented audience.
The Argus Clearinghouse (formerly The Clearinghouse for Subject-Oriented Internet Resource Guides)	**http://www.clearinghouse.net/**	Excellent starting point for research guides on the Net by subject area. Research and university audience.

ganizes Web resources by category. A directory will give you an overview of what's out there, and you may find that someone else has already done your work for you by organizing materials in your area of interest. To find environmental law resources, we could start with the GNN Whole Internet Catalog; after browsing through their list of topic categories, we choose **Government and Politics**. This in turn provides us with a link to **Law**, and on the law page, we find **Environmental Law around the World** organized by EcoNet. This strategy has the advantage of taking us directly to a number of related resources, and if we have confidence in those who have collected these resources, we will have easily and quickly accomplished our research goals.

However, directories also have disadvantages. First of all, no directory can ever be fully comprehensive. When directories are compiled by a central company, such as GNN or EINet, they are only as good as the time and resources the company is willing to put into their development. Directories are also biased according to the purposes and perspective of the organizer; for example, the Yahoo index is tailored to suit a popular audience. And unless you know the history of the directory and the strategies for its upkeep, you never know whether it's up-to-date or suffers from linkrot. Part of the trick is knowing which directories are more reliable, and the ones listed here will generally provide you good starting points for your research. (When typing in the URLs in the **Location line** of your Web client, remember that URLs are case sensitive: use upper- and lower-case characters as given.)

4.2 The Spider's Catch: Using Web Search Engines

Sometimes your topic of research won't fit neatly into one of the categories that directories provide, or you'll find that the directories don't give you the specific information you need. In these cases, Web search engines are useful. Search engines that cover the entire Web will give you more comprehensive and up-to-date results than directories can offer. The search engines accomplish this by sending out network robot programs, often called "crawlers" or "spiders," that search the contents of all publicly accessible Web, Gopher, and FTP servers, and then compile enormous indices of the words in all of the files. (Netscape users can jump to a Web search, and a list of search engines, from the top menu bar; choose **Directory** | **Internet Search**.)

When we use a search engine like Lycos, we are in fact searching the index that the Lycos spider has compiled. It would be impossible to search the entire Web in a reasonable amount of time (robots generally take several days to work their way around the world), but this ongoing indexing allows us to come very close to a comprehensive search of the Web. Since the Web is dynamic and always changing, each new Web crawl by a spider results in a new index of content.

Web search engines all operate differently. They use different robots and indexing programs to compile their data, different syntax in their search forms, and different criteria for prioritizing the results they send back to the user. You will find that to search for more sophisticated combinations of words and to use Boolean operators like "and," "or," and "but not," you'll need to read the search help pages to find out how a particular search engine handles the logic of a query. You'll also find that different search engines will return different results even if you use the same combinations of keywords, since they have various strategies for indexing and prioritizing results. If you need to do a comprehensive search and find *everything* available on the Web on a given topic, you should use several different engines and compare the results. (A convenient way to send the same search to several search engines at once is to use SavvySearch or Search.com, listed in "Information Site 6," on pages 62–63.)

As with directories, the results delivered by a particular search engine will be only as good as the engine. Generally, the size of the index is a good indication of the comprehensiveness of the search; bigger is better. Smarter, more sophisticated search engines are in the beginning stages of development. Increasingly, you can expect to see search engines that will give you confidence ratings on the results they return, conceptual searches, and options that will allow you to customize searches to meet your specific needs. Search engines can't make intellectual judgments for you, but to the extent that mechanical features can help yield better results, we should see real improvements in search engines in the near future. Other innovations on the client side, such as personal agents that will work with your Web client program and tailor searches to match your Web browsing behavior, are now emerging on the marketplace (see Chapter 7).

More-sophisticated search engines will help alleviate some of the drawbacks of using these tools for research. Currently, you will find that any given keyword search is likely to return thousands of hits, which would take hours, if not days, to sort. Tailoring the search query with keyword combinations can help narrow the field, but culling through and evaluating the usefulness of the results is still likely to be very time-consuming. The openness of the Web and the mechanical nature of search engines often lead to results that will give you congressional reports and a fan's "Nine Inch Nails" home page side by side,

INFORMATION SITE 6

SEARCH ENGINES

Name	URL	Comments
Netscape's Net Search Directory	**http://home.netscape.com/home/internet-search.html** Or click on **Directory | Internet Search**	Netscape's handy jump station for access to Web search engines. Good starting point for experimenting with searches.
Lycos	**http://www.lycos.com/**	Indexes over 90% of the Web. Allows customized searches. Fast and reliable. Indexes FTP and Gopher sites too, but not Usenet Newsgroups.
Inktomi	**http://inktomi.berkeley.edu/**	Fast. Uses multiple servers and parallel processing. Allows efficient searches of multiple keywords.
Alta Vista	**http://www.altavista.digital.com/**	Fast. Project sponsored by Digital Equipment Corporation (DEC). Also searches Usenet Newsgroups.
Excite	**http://www.excite.com/**	Large index of Web files, searchable by concept and by keywords. Also searches Usenet Newsgroups and Usenet classifieds.

with no explanation of the relative value or reliability of either. The burdens of judgment and analysis are on the researcher. (Smarter search engines, personal intelligent agents, and information filtering software are now being developed to make finding relevant information easier; see Chapter 7.)

4.3 Search Tools on Specific Websites

Whenever you use a search tool on the Web, you need to understand what you are searching, that is, what the search engine

Name	URL	Comments
InfoSeek	**http://www2.infoseek.com/Query**	Reliable search engine. Searches by keyword, concept, and related terms. Also searches Usenet Newsgroups.
HotBot	**http://www.hotbot.com/**	Search engine developed by *HotWired* using Inktomi's parallel processing technology. Fast. HotBot makes claims to be the most comprehensive index of the Web.
SavvySearch	**http://www.cs.colostate.edu/~dreiling/smartform.html**	Allows searches with several engines simultaneously. Also has international language capabilities.
All-In-One Search Page	**http://www.albany.net/allinone/**	Very useful compilation of search forms for all Web search engines. Find information, people, software, and reference works from one Web site.
Search.com (by C|Net)	**http://www.search.com/**	A useful all-in-one search page with multiple forms for many search engines.

INFORMATION SITE 7

SEARCHABLE SUBJECT-SPECIFIC WEBSITES

Name	URL	Comments
Open Market's Commercial Web Sites Index	**http://www.directory.net/**	Master index of all businesses and corporations on the Web.
Smithsonian Natural History Museum	**http://nmnhwww.si.edu/nmnhweb.html**	Indexed guide to research resources at the museum.
CERN Particle Physics Laboratory	**http://www.cern.ch/** **http://www.cern.ch/CERN/Search.html**	Searchable database of physics research at CERN.
Voice of the Shuttle Humanities Server	**http://humanitas.ucsb.edu/**	Large searchable index of information in the humanities (literature, art, history, philosophy).
Telecommunications resources on the Internet (University of Michigan)	**http://www.spp.umich.edu/telecom/telecom-info.html**	Large searchable database of telecommunications information and businesses.
The Labyrinth: Medieval Studies Web Site (Georgetown University)	**http://www.georgetown.edu/labyrinth**	Search all files on medieval history, literature, art, and philosophy.
Legal Information Institute (Cornell University)	**http://www.law.cornell.edu/topical.html**	One of the best searchable indices for law information.
Social Sciences (WWW Virtual Library)	**http://coombs.anu.edu.au/WWWVL-SocSci.html**	Searchable index of all Web resources in the social sciences.
U.S. government legislative information (Thomas)	**http://thomas.loc.gov/**	Searchable database of all legislation in the U.S. Congress.

software does with its index. Some search engines like those listed in "Information Site 6" compile indices from the entire Internet, but others are set up to provide searches of a particular site or set of resources. Sometimes these narrower search tools can offer a good combination of reliability and manageability. For example, the *Voice of the Shuttle* Website organizes resources in the humanities (**http://humanitas.ucsb.edu/**). This site is coordinated by Alan Liu at the University of California at Santa Barbara, and given the Website organizer's credentials and his criteria for including materials in this site, we can be reasonably confident that what we will find here is reliable and has scholarly value. The *Voice of the Shuttle* includes a search tool that will search all of the material included in its organizational structure. When we use this search tool, we need to recognize that we are not doing a comprehensive search of the entire Web, but searching only this site's collection of resources. Searches of the *Voice of the Shuttle* could either take us directly to the materials we need or provide us with useful ways of narrowing our search before we go to global search engines. Many corporate and government Websites have search engines for materials on their specific sites, allowing quick access to specific information.

Conscientious Web developers identify the range of their search tools, telling users that they are searching only a particular body of information or set of files. If you are uncertain of what the search tool is doing, you should be cautious about the comprehensiveness of the results. Here are some usefully organized subject-specific Websites with search engines for locally indexed materials.

4.4 Searching Individual Files

A final level of searching allows you to locate a particular word or phrase in a specific file. Often the files you find when conducting broad searches of the Web will yield the information you need in an obvious way, such as giving you an alphabetical list of senators. However, sometimes you will need a fine-tooth comb to sort through the information in a specific file. Web client programs provide built-in "search" or "find" tools that allow you to do a keyword search of the file that you are currently viewing. For example, the legal classified job listings will provide you with a file that lists 83 openings in corporate law; you could browse through this file to see the range of positions, or you could click on the **Find** button in Netscape to search this file for the keyword "Boston," or the phrase "real estate" to take you directly to the listings of interest (**http://www.lawjobs.com/nyjobs.html**). This level of searching will only tell you what is in one specific file at a time, the file you are currently viewing with your Web client program. The **Find** or **Search** button on your Web client program will *not* search for a keyword or phrase in any other files out on the Web. Nonetheless, when the specific file before you is large or complex, the Web client's finding tool will save valuable time.

4.5 Using Online Library Catalogs and Databases

A search of library holdings on a topic is usually the first place to begin a research project. This remains true even in an era of digital information. Until the contents of most print records are transferred to digital storage, books and print media will continue to be our deepest record of information and knowledge. But we no longer need to use only books or print materials to study what's in print. Many texts are now found in electronic form, and soon many journals will be available only electronically and delivered over the Net. Rather than skimming through drawers of index cards or print bibliographies, we can now use searchable databases of library materials in a fraction of the time it took to do searches the old way.

Electronic storage has changed the ways libraries use space and resources, and library science has undergone a great transformation in the past two decades. Librarians have been at the

USER NOTE
LIBRARIES AND COMPUTER RECORDS

In 1965 the Library of Congress developed the MARC (Machine-Readable Cataloging) format, which provided a standard hardware-independent cataloging method for all kinds of media. Libraries can now easily catalog everything from books and videos to electronic texts and CDs. Since 1971, librarians also have been able to exchange information about holdings through OCLC, an online library database that uses the MARC format. OCLC now contains the records of over 20,000 libraries in 60 countries worldwide. Most of the Internet-accessible library catalogs are in MARC format, and thus libraries on the Net integrate two open and hardware-independent systems. Today, some of the best access to Net and Web resources is provided by libraries.

forefront of new developments in information technology, and they now see their role as information access providers in the widest sense. The Internet has created a new information environment, and the catalogs and collections of thousands of libraries are now accessible via the Net and Web.

Some libraries have developed Web interfaces to their catalogs, which allow Web users the convenience of interactive forms for search queries and other data access. Most library connections, however, are established through an open or publicly accessible telnet session with a library's computer. There are several kinds of proprietary database software for library catalogs, and the telnet connection allows a user to run this software from anywhere on the Internet. With the telnet link, a user gives commands, inserts search data, or chooses options from a menu that perform operations on the library's remote computer system.

Telnet connections are almost always done in text-only mode, and usually in what is known as "VT–100 terminal emulation," meaning that your computer interacts with the library's system as if it were an industry-standard nongraphical terminal, the VT–100. In VT–100 mode, we use only the standard keyboard characters and a few special commands (like **Escape** and **Control** key sequences).

Telnet links to libraries can be confusing until you become familiar with the kinds of database software that library systems use. Most libraries provide user-friendly interfaces to their systems, with help screens and command syntax listed on the screen; but often you'll never know what software package

WEBSITES FOR HYTELNET: TELNET LINKS TO ALL LIBRARIES

Owner	URL
University of Saskatchewan Libraries	**http://moondog.usask.ca/hytelnet/**
Nova Southeastern University (Florida)	**http://www.nova.edu/Inter-Links/hytelnet.html**
University of Cambridge (England)	**http://www.cam.ac.uk/Hytelnet/index.html**
University of Western Australia	**http://www.library.uwa.edu.au/libweb/hytelnet**

you'll be dumped into when you log on to the library's system until after you're there. Another difficulty with telnet sessions is that there is no one set of commands for logging in and logging off a system.

Luckily, there is online help for using all the Internet-accessible library catalogs and databases. Hytelnet, a directory of worldwide libraries developed by Peter Scott at the University of Saskatchewan Libraries, provides links to all the libraries on the Internet and information about how to use each library's database software. With Hytelnet, you can review a screen of information about the commands used for doing searches before you make the telnet connection to the database server. There are several Web interfaces to the Hytelnet directories and links; make sure you have a telnet client program configured to work with Netscape before making the Web link to the Hytelnet sites (see Chapter 7).

Using your Web client, you can also go to the Libraries page in Daedalus's Guides to the Web. This is a page of links to the major research libraries in the United States. Simply click on the library links and start your telnet session.

INFORMATION SITE 9

MAJOR RESEARCH LIBRARIES ON THE INTERNET

Name	URL
Daedalus's Guides to the Web: Libraries	**http://www.georgetown.edu/labyrinth/library/library_catalogues.html**
Libweb: Library Servers via the Web	**http://sunsite.berkeley.edu/Libweb/**

WEB INTERFACES TO LIBRARIES

Library	URL
Eric Morgan's directory of libraries with web interfaces (North Carolina State University)	**http://www.lib.ncsu.edu/staff/morgan/alcuin/wwwed-catalogs.html**
University of California at San Diego, web interface (with hypertext links to *Encyclopaedia Britannica* entries)	**http://pactech.ucsd.edu/screens/opacmenu.html**
Case Western Reserve library	**http://catalog.cwru.edu/search/**
Iowa State University library	**http://www.lib.iastate.edu/scholar/icat.html**
University of Utrecht library (Netherlands)	**http://www.ubu.ruu.nl/**

The number of libraries with Web interfaces will continue to grow, as MARC databases become accessible through Web server technology. For a glimpse of what's to come and some fully functional library databases on the Web, see above.

5 Tracking, Managing, and Citing Resources on the Web

The Web has become an indispensable research tool for all kinds of writing projects. This chapter will provide some tips for tracking and managing the information you've found, and guidelines for citing and documenting the information sources in your own writing. It will also point out the intellectual property and copyright issues involved with using electronic information.

5.1 Bookmarks and Annotations: Saving Links to Visited Websites

As you explore the Web, you will quickly find that you need ways to organize the resources you've found and the sites you want to revisit. Generally it is *not* a good idea to write down URLs, since they are long and abstract and then must be retyped exactly in order to work. Fortunately, Windows and Mac copy and paste features and tools such as the bookmarks organizer built into Netscape and other Web clients make it easy to compile information electronically as you are working.

A bookmarks file is a list of URLs with a title for each link. Most Web client programs include a bookmarks tool that allows you to save URLs in a bookmarks file for future use. A bookmarks list makes it easy to revisit sites that you have found useful, since you can simply click on an item in the list and go directly to the site, without typing in the URL or remembering how you got to it before. Generally, the bookmarks file will automatically include additional information such as when the bookmark was added to the list, when it was last visited, and the title of the Web file. Most bookmarks tools provide options for adding your own annotations and organizing bookmarks into folders.

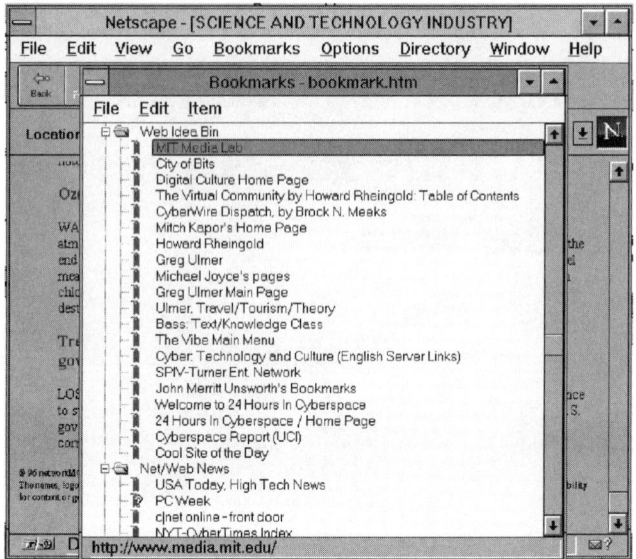

***Netscape Navigator* Bookmarks window.**

Compiling a bookmarks list is easy in Netscape: when you find a Website that you want to revisit later, simply go to the **Bookmarks** menu and choose **Add Bookmark**. This will add the URL of the file you are currently viewing to the bookmarks file. As you add bookmarks, you may wish to make notes to yourself, such as bibliographical information, a description of the resource, or comments on how you plan to use it later. To make annotations, go to the **Bookmarks** menu, choose **Go to Bookmarks**, click once on the item you want to annotate, and choose **Properties** from the **Item** menu. This will display the full information about the item, including a space for your own description of the item. Information you add here could prove useful later, especially if you are doing research and plan to cite this Web file as a source.

As you compile bookmarks and the list starts to grow, you may wish to organize your bookmarks into separate folders. Netscape makes it easy: go to the **Bookmarks** menu, choose **Go to Bookmarks**, click once on the spot where you want to add a folder, then choose **Insert Folder** from the **Item** menu. Once you've created folders (for example, folders corresponding to various research topics), you can drag and drop items in your bookmarks list into the appropriate folders. Folders can be nested within folders to organize materials into categories within a larger project. You can also use the **Sort Bookmarks** option under the **Item** menu to sort your bookmarks and folders alphabetically.

The bookmarks file, including any annotations or organizing you have done, will be saved to the hard drive of the computer on which you are working. If you are in a situation where you do not have sole access to the computer—maybe you work in a lab or share the computer with colleagues—your bookmarks file can be saved to a disk. When you have compiled a bookmarks file during a working session, you can take this file with you by choosing **Save As** from the **File** menu in the bookmarks window and then specifying the drive where you've inserted your disk. Give the file a name and save it to the disk. (The file can be called whatever you like, as long as it has an **.htm** or **.html** extension (for example, research.htm); this will make it possible to load the file into Netscape later. The bookmarks file you have saved to disk can be used in Netscape on any compatible computer simply by choosing **Open File** under the **File** menu in the bookmarks window or from the main screen. These options give you the freedom to take your bookmarks with you wherever you go, from home to work, from lab to lab, from the library to the office. You can also share your bookmarks with others simply by giving them a copy of your bookmarks file.

USER NOTE
BOOKMARK SHORTCUTS FOR NETSCAPE

Action	How-To
Save URL for future reference	Click on **Bookmarks** | **Add Bookmark**
Organize your bookmark file	• Click on **Bookmarks** | **Go to Bookmarks** • To annotate or rename a bookmark, click on **Item** | **Properties** • To divide your bookmark list into folders, click on **Item** | **Insert Folder** • To reorganize the list, highlight, drag, and drop the item to a new place in the list

5.2 Web Research Shortcuts

The multitasking feature of Windows and Macintosh systems—the ability to have multiple program windows open on the screen simultaneously—makes it easy to copy and paste material from window to window when you do research on the Web. Here are some tips for streamlining research in a windowed Internet environment. As a general rule, do *not* write things down; copy and move information within the electronic environment. This will increase your efficiency and accuracy when managing information on the Web.

USER NOTE
COPY AND PASTE SHORTCUTS FOR WEB FILES

Action	How-To
Copy a URL from the **Location** line and paste it into a word processor text file	1. Highlight the URL in the **Location line** (click on the line or drag the mouse across URL box). 2. Press **control-c** or click on **Edit** | **Copy** (to copy it). 3. Toggle to the word processor window. 4. Press **control-v** or click on **Edit** | **Paste** to insert (paste) the URL into the file.
Copy text from a Web file into a word processor text file.	1. Highlight the section of text to be copied (use the mouse). 2. Press **control-c** or click on **Edit** | **Copy** (to copy it). 3. Toggle to the word processor window. 4. Press **control-v** or click on **Edit** | **Paste** to insert (paste) the copied text into the file.
Copy text or a URL between an email message and a word processor text file	1. Highlight the section of text to be copied (use the mouse) in the text file or the email message. 2. Press **control-c** or click on **Edit** | **Copy** (to copy it). 3. Toggle to the word processor (or email) window. 4. Press **control-v** or click on **Edit** | **Paste** to insert (paste) the copied text into the file

Copy and Paste URLs and Text into Your Word Processor or Email Editor

As you do research on the Web, you can streamline your work by using the copy and paste features that allow you to transfer text quickly from any Windows or Mac program to any other program. For example, if you are writing a research paper, memo, or article, open your word processing program while you are using your Web client program. You can easily toggle back and forth between these programs to copy and paste material rather than retyping it. (In Windows, **Alt-Tab** allows you

Action	How-To
Copy text or a URL between an email message and the **Location** line	1. Highlight the URL to be copied (use the mouse). 2. Press **control-c** or click on **Edit** | **Copy** (to copy it). 3. Toggle to the Web client (or email) window. 4. Press **control-v** or click on **Edit** | **Paste** to insert (paste) the URL in the Location line (or email message).
Advanced users: copy sections of the HTML source file into a text document or an HTML file that you are editing	1. In Netscape, click on **View** | **Document Source**. 2. Drag the mouse to highlight the section of the file to be copied. 3. Press **control-c** to copy. 4. Toggle to the word processor file or HTML editor file. 5. Press **control-v** to insert (paste) the copied text into the file.

to toggle among active windows on the screen. You can also arrange your screen so that windows overlap; simply click on a portion of an underlying window to make it the active window on the screen. In Windows 95, your open windows appear at the bottom of the screen; toggle among them by clicking on the one you want to be active.)

For example, if you have found a file on the Web that you want to quote in your research paper, use the mouse in the Netscape window to highlight and copy the portion of the report that you want to quote, then go to your word processing program and paste the text you have copied directly into the research paper. (Put the quoted text in quotation marks or format it as a block, indented quote in your research paper.) Then go back to Netscape, compile the bibliographical information you need for properly citing the source (author, title, publisher, publication date, URL, and date cited; see section 5.3), and copy this information into your paper. You now have a correctly quoted and properly cited source without having to write down or retype the text or bibliographical information.

If you avoid writing down URLs and the information you find on the Web, you'll avoid errors. For example, if a colleague sends you a URL in an email message, you can copy the URL out of the message and paste it directly into the **Location** box in Netscape. (Highlight it and copy it in the email window; highlight or delete an existing URL in the Netscape **Location box**, then use **control**-v or **Edit** | **Paste** to insert the copied URL in the **Location box**.) You can reverse the process to email a URL to someone else, or you can use the **Mail Document** option under the **File** menu to email the entire document to anyone, including yourself. Use the same method for any URLs that you see quoted or mentioned in any other Net or Web file.

Be creative in using these shortcuts to facilitate your own research and writing strategies; they can help you avoid inaccurate quotations and typos. In all cases, however, make sure you enclose anything you quote from a Web file in quotation marks (or use an indented block quote), and always compile the bibliographical information for the Web sources as you go; otherwise you will later find it extremely difficult or even impossible to document your sources.

Saving Web Files to Disk

You may find that you want to use these strategies to copy blocks of text from Web files into a word processing file while making notes to yourself for use later. Or you can save an entire file to disk for future reference by using the **Save As** option under the **File** menu in Netscape. You can use the original file name (the one in the URL) as a default, or you can rename the file anything you wish. Make sure to give the file a **.htm/.html** extension if you rename it. When you have saved Web files to disk, you can view them again in Netscape by using the **Open File** option under the **File** menu, and then change to the drive where you've put the file (usually "a:" for the diskette drive).

Inline images are separate files; if you need to include them for future reference, you should save them to your disk separately. (There are various ways of indicating how to insert images in an HTML file; often the full URL with complete directory path is omitted, and when you view the file locally from your own disk, Netscape won't be able to find the image file.)

These and other strategies that you can devise to suit your own needs will save you valuable time and energy. By using the copy, paste, and save options, you'll be sure that the electronically transferred materials exactly match their originals.

5.3 Citing Electronic Sources from the Internet

The tools for organizing, compiling, and copying material from the Web and the Internet keep improving and getting more sophisticated, but mechanical tools cannot substitute for your own judgment and responsibility for accurately and ethically citing your sources. As with traditional research methods, you must always keep track of where you got your information, whether you have quoted exactly or paraphrased, and how a reader can subsequently find your sources. The Internet provides an additional challenge, because unlike print sources that are relatively stable, Internet sources are dynamic and constantly changing. This necessitates recording not only where you found materials, but also when. Always make a note of the date when you downloaded or quoted material from an Internet source, and include that date as part of your citation.

In general, you will find that citing Internet resources follows the same basic rules as the citation style you are accustomed to using. You will include author, title, and publication information, to the extent that this information is available. In addition, you will include the date you accessed the resource and the specifics of its online availability; a URL is generally the best way of specifying the online availability of an Internet source.

It is important to be consistent in your citation style throughout a research paper or article. Standard handbooks for citation, such as the *MLA Handbook* (Modern Languages Association) and the *Publication Manual of the American Psychological Association* (APA), include more detailed guidelines for citing various types of electronic resources, including some that are not explained here, such as CD-ROMs.

Before you begin your research, it's a good idea to find out from your instructor, employer, or publisher exactly what citation style you should be using, since this will determine what bibliographical information you should compile as you're working. Because the world of online resources is expanding and changing rapidly, style guides (like MLA, APA, and others) cannot keep up with these changes in their published guidelines; thus citation standards are in a state of flux. Existing guidelines generally have not made the transition from the logic of print technology to the logic of Internet technology, and so you may find that some of the standard citation "rules" are contradictory or don't apply to digital information sources.

For a useful overview of styles for electronic resources, see Maurice Crouse's online article "Citing Electronic Information in History Papers," and the online guides by Xia Li and Nancy Crane (URLs below). The best print source for citations styles is Li and Crane's *Electronic Styles: An Expanded Guide to Citing Electronic Information* (1996).[1] Similar guidelines are also available in the online document by Janice Walker, which is endorsed by the Alliance for Computers and Writing. The authors of these documents update them as new standards are accepted, so the guidelines reflect the dynamic state of the Net.

MLA Documentation

MLA documentation style consists of two parts: *in-text citations*, which include basic information that refers to a list of *works cited* at the end of the document.[2]

IN-TEXT CITATIONS For print sources, the in-text citation generally requires two pieces of information: the name of the author or title of the source and the page reference. For Internet

1. Xia Li and Nancy B. Crane, *Electronic Style: A Guide to Citing Electronic Information* (Westport, Conn.: Mecklermedia, 1996). Li and Crane are reference librarians at the University of Vermont at Burlington and have been influential in the expansion of both the MLA and the APA guidelines for citing electronic sources.

2. Summarized from Joseph Gibaldi, *MLA Handbook for Writers of Research Papers*, 4th ed. (New York: Modern Language Association of America, 1995).

sources, the second is usually omitted, since Internet files do not have page numbers, unless they are duplicating a print source. The purpose of the in-text citation is to refer readers to the list of works cited, so if the name of the author or the title of the source is clear, you do not need to repeat this information in parentheses. If the reference is not clear in context, provide this information in parentheses at the end of the sentence that contains information or a quotation from the source. (Note that the parenthetical reference is included inside the period but outside the quotation marks.)

Examples

> In *Computer Networking: Global Infrastructure for the 21st Century*, Vinton Cerf notes that the "1994 data communications market approached roughly $15 billion/year."

> As we analyze the impact of the information age on global economies, we should consider the fact that the "1994 data communications market approached roughly $15 billion/year" (Cerf).

In each of these examples, the in-text citation refers the reader to the list of works cited, where the author provides full information about the source.

WORKS CITED LIST The "Works Cited" list includes individual entries with detailed bibliographical information for each of the works you have cited. These entries are arranged in alphabetical order by the author's last name (or by the title if the

GUIDES FOR CITING INTERNET SOURCES

Name	URL
Janice Walker's MLA/Alliance for Computers and Writing Style Guide	**http://library.ccsu.ctstateu.edu/~history/walker.html**
Xia Li and Nancy Crane's Guide to MLA Citation Style	**http://www.uvm.edu/~xli/reference/mla.html**
Xia Li and Nancy Crane's Guide to APA Citation Style	**http://www.uvm.edu/~xli/reference/apa.html**
Maurice Crouse's Citing Electronic Information in History Papers	**http://www.people.memphis.edu/~crousem/elcite.html**

author is not known). The first line of each entry is flush left and subsequent lines are indented five spaces, or approximately ½ inch. Leave a blank line between entries.

Entries for Internet sources should include the following information, if available: author, title, publication information, name of computer network (i.e., the Internet), date of access, and specific information indicating online availability (e.g., the URL). Note that you should not put a period after a URL, since this could be confusing. The type of information included in your citation entries will vary somewhat, depending on the nature of the source.

Examples

For *online publications adapted from a print publication,* include publication information for the original print publication along with the online version.

Littleton, C. Scott, and Linda A. Malcor. "Some Notes on Merlin." *Arthuriana* 5.3 (1995): 87–95. Online. Internet. 2 Mar. 1996. Available: http://dc.smu.edu/Arthuriana/littleton.html

For *Online publications with no printed analog or none specified,* include online publication information, if available. See the *MLA Handbook* for detailed guidelines pertaining to various types of resources within this category.

Cerf, Vinton. *Computer Networking: Global Infrastructure for the 21st Century*. Computing Research Association, 1995. Online. Internet. 26 Feb. 1996. Available: http://www.cs.washington.edu/homes/lazowska/cra/networks.html

For *Email communications or newsgroup postings,* include the name of the author, a description, the recipient (for email), the date of the communication or posting, and the location where you found the communication if you were not the original recipient.

Cohen, Jeffrey. Email to Interscripta discussion list. 25 Oct. 1993. Online. Internet. 15 Feb. 1996. Available: http://www.mun.ca/lists/interscripta/interscripta.log9310d

APA Documentation

APA documentation consists of two parts: in-text citations, which include basic information, and the references list at the end of the document, which includes more complete bibliographical information.[3]

IN-TEXT CITATIONS For print sources, the in-text citation generally requires three pieces of information: the name of the author or the first two or three words of the title, the date of publication, and the page reference. For Internet sources, the third is usually omitted, since Internet files do not have page numbers, unless they are duplicating a print source. The purpose of the in-text citation is to refer readers to the references list (with the exception of email citations), so if the name of the author or the title of the source is clear, you only need to provide the date of publication in parentheses. If the author's name or the title of the source is not clear in context, provide this information and the date of publication in parentheses at the end of the sentence that contains information or a quotation from the source. Note that the parenthetical reference is included inside the period but outside the quotation marks.

Email correspondence and postings to news groups and bulletin boards are treated as personal communications, and thus are cited in the text but are not included in the references list.

Examples

For *Internet files*:

> In *Computer Networking: Global Infrastructure for the 21st Century*, Vinton Cerf notes that the "1994 data communications market approached roughly $15 billion/year" (1995).
>
> As we analyze the impact of the information age on global economies, we should consider the fact that the "1994 data communications market approached roughly $15 billion/year" (Cerf, 1995).

For *Email*:

> Jeffrey Cohen provided a useful overview of medieval masculinities in his opening statement to the

3. Summarized from American Psychological Association, *Publication Manual of the American Psychological Association*, 4th ed. (Washington, D.C.: American Psychological Association, 1994).

Interscripta list (Email communication, October 25, 1993).

References List

The references list includes individual entries with detailed bibliographical information for each of the works you have cited (excluding email messages and other personal communications). These entries are arranged in alphabetical order by the author's last name (or by the title if the author is not known). For final copy, APA recommends that the first line of each entry be flush left and subsequent lines indented five spaces, or approximately ½ inch. Leave a blank line between entries.

Entries for Internet sources should include the following information, if available: author, date of publication or last revision (if unknown, provide date of access), title, the type of electronic medium (e.g., "On-line" or "On-line serial"), and specific information for retrieving the material (e.g., the URL). The type of information included will vary somewhat, depending on the nature of the source.

Examples

Cerf, V. (1995). *Computer networking: Global infrastructure for the 21st century* [On-line]. Available: http://www.cs.washington.edu/homes/lazowska/cra/networks.html

Barnett, W. P. (1995). Modeling internal organizational change. *Annual Review of Sociology*. [On-line abstract], *21*. Available: http://www.annurev.org/series/sociolgy/Vol21/so21abst.htm#barnett

APA guidelines do not require the date of finding for the Internet source. This is a deficiency in the APA citation format, and an indication that the guidelines have yet to adapt to networked electronic information.

5.4 Intellectual Property, Copyright, Fair Use, and Electronic Plagiarism

General rules about copyright and intellectual property in print and other media apply to using sources on the Internet. There are three issues to consider:

- Observing copyright and respecting others' intellectual property when applicable.
- Practicing and observing fair use when applicable.
- Understanding the ethical and rhetorical aspects of proper citation of sources.

The Internet often seems to obscure the boundaries of ownership and authorship because it is easy to copy material, paste together pieces of others' work, and call a resulting text or image one's own. Some materials on the Net are openly in the public domain and have no clear attributions to authors. Client–server file transfers and the ability to download a copy of anything publicly available on the Internet raises the important, basic question "What is a copy?" (and even "What is an original?") in the digital age. We might also ask "How much does one need to alter a work copied from the Internet before it becomes another work or before one can legitimately call it one's own?" Similarly, the principle of fair use for purposes of research, commentary, and education places limits on the exclusive rights of a copyright owner. It will take many years before these issues are resolved both in the courts and in common practice, but until there's any consensus or clear legal guidelines, we should rely on current principles of respect for intellectual property, fair use guidelines for research and education, and the ethics of documenting sources of information.

In general, treat others property, including online resources, as you would have others treat your own. Always document your sources regardless of the medium: Web files, electronic images, sound and video clips, and email messages all have authors that should be acknowledged when you include these materials in your own work (for citation guidelines, see section 5.3.). Respect others' work: do not use others' work as your own, and do not alter it without their permission. Remember that copyright is implied in electronic publications even if it is not explicitly stated: a text, artistic work, or compilation of resources is the property of the author/creator from the moment of its publication. Registering a work with the government copyright office is not required for copyright law.

We must also feel free to practice fair use for education and research and not be intimidated by often exclusive claims made on material by copyright holders. They have rights, and so do researchers, students, educators, and writers. The U.S. Copyright Act, section 107 on fair use, states that copyrighted works may be used "for purposes such as criticism, com-

INFORMATION SITE 12

COPYRIGHT ISSUES

Name	URL	Comments
U.S. Copyright Act of 1971 (amended 1994)	**http://www.law.cornell.edu/usc/17/overview.html**	A hypertext edition of the act, hosted by Cornell University Law School
U.S. Copyright Office, Library of Congress	**http://marvel.loc.gov/copyright/**	Provides basic copyright information and searchable Copyright Office records.
Thomas: Library of Congress Legislative Information	**http://thomas.loc.gov/**	Search for and read recent and pending legislation on copyright and intellectual property.
Cornell University, Legal Information Institute: copyright information on the Net	**http://www.law.cornell.edu/topics/copyright.html**	Best resource for primary sources of copyright law.
Association of Research Libraries: copyright and intellectual property documents	**http://arl.cni.org/scomm/copyright/copyright.html**	Excellent set of resources for understanding the lawful use of copyrighted materials for research and education.
The Report ("White Paper") of the Information Infrastructure Task Force (IITF) on Intellectual Property	**http://www.uspto.gov/web/ipnii/**	Rationale for intellectual property law as it applies to the Internet and makes recommendations to Congress on how to adapt the law to technological changes.
Critique of the IITF White Paper	**http://www.hotwired.com/wired/whitepaper.html**	Analysis and critique of copyright issues by Pamela Samuelson, a leading copyright lawyer.

ment, news reporting, teaching (including multiple copies for classroom use), scholarship, or research" (**http://www.law.cornell.edu/usc/17/107.html**). Interpretations vary, but a general rule to follow is that making copies of copyrighted works, in whole or in part, is not a copyright infringement if an author adds new interpretation, commentary, or criticism for research or teaching and if such copies do not adversely affect the market for or value of the copyrighted work. This interpretation also assumes that the use of the copyrighted material is for nonprofit educational and personal research purposes. These general guidelines allow for a fairly liberal use of materials on the Internet, but intellectual property should always be respected, especially when citing or using copyrighted material for fair use purposes. When using materials legitimately under fair use protection for research and education, remember to document sources and attribute all works to their authors whenever possible.

There is also an important, and often overlooked, rhetorical and ethical dimension to the use and citation of sources. Writers of research papers, reports, and articles should include full citations for the electronic sources they have used in their work, just as they would for print sources. Using the citation conventions of your field or profession demonstrates your attention to professional standards and to the expectations of your audience. Inexperienced and unskilled writers often don't realize that properly documenting their sources enhances the credibility and authority of their writing and distinguishes informed, well-researched writing from casual or poorly argued

FAIR USE PRACTICES AND GUIDELINES

Content	URL
The Fair Use Limitation of Exclusive Rights, sec. 107 of the U.S. Copyright Act	**http://www.law.cornell.edu/usc/17/107.html**
Fair use documents and case studies for copyrighted materials in a college course database	**http://www.geom.umn.edu/docs/education/chance/Fair_Use/fair.html**
Consortium of College and University Media Centers: fair use guidelines	**http://www-act.ucsd.edu/webad/fairuse.html**

work. If you are unsure about the method of citation to use, ask for guidance from a professor or from an experienced writer in your organization. Plagiarized writing is almost always found out because informed professionals in all fields know who's doing what and how ideas circulate; only immature and ignorant people think they can get away with plagiarizing from print or digital sources.

The volatile topics of copyright, intellectual property, and fair use in the information age have generated a great deal of debate. Concerned Netizens should study the latest publications, recommendations, and legislation as they appear online. The following sites provide useful starting points.

6
Off the Web but in Your Interface: Email and Interactive Communications

There are other forms of computer-mediated interactive communication on the Net, and although they are off the Web in the technical sense (that is, they are not part of the Web's client–server multimedia system), *Netscape Navigator* and other Web clients now provide a user interface for other forms of Net communications. A full description of all the forms of computer-mediated communication on the Net is beyond the scope of this book, but this chapter provides an overview of how you can use Netscape (and, increasingly, other Web software) as your Net interface for email and multi-user communications environments. (In Netscape, help is always available for these features in the online users' *Handbook*. Click on **Help | Handbook** in the top menu bar.)

6.1 Using Netscape for Email

You probably learned to do email before being introduced to the Web, but if not, this book isn't intended to be a guide to learning basic Internet email. (There are lots of good books on email; but having a friend walk you through the steps is the best way to begin.) There are many ways to do Internet email, and you may want to continue to use email separately by logging in to whatever computer system you currently use. *Netscape Navigator,* however, can act as a convenient front end to email communication by allowing you to access email from the mail server you currently use, or from a new email account that comes with your Internet service provider's package (see Chapter 3). Netscape has a built-in email program, a version of *Eudora,* a popular GUI program. The Netscape email program can be configured to fetch email and post messages through a connection with any mail server you have an account on. Netscape will launch a separate window for email, and you can keep it open during your Internet session to monitor new messages as they come in.

You need to configure Netscape for email by using the **Options | Mail and News Preferences** menu. Enter all the required information in the dialogue boxes in each page of the **Mail and News Preferences** section. You will need to know the name of the mail server where you have your email account (usually the Internet host name after the "@" sign in your email address), or if you are using SLIP/PPP from an ISP, you need to enter the ISP's mail server name.

When you have properly configured Netscape, you can launch an email window any time by clicking on the small envelope icon in the lower right of the *Netscape Navigator* window, or by clicking on **Window | Netscape Mail** in the top menu bar.

You can leave email and *Netscape Navigator* windows open throughout your work session, and you may find that working this way allows you to use information from both sources in a more integrated way. An extremely useful feature of Netscape's email program is that any URLs cited in an email message are turned into highlighted hotlinks, which you can click on to view the files as you would with any other Web document. Netscape fetches the file in the URL cited in the email message and displays it in the *Netscape Navigator* window in one step. With the GUI interface, furthermore, you can always copy and paste information from and to your email messages, a feature that comes in handy when you want to cite URLs or copy other Web information from or to an email message.

6.2 Using Netscape for Usenet Newsgroups

Usenet Newsgroups, or discussion groups, constitute one of the oldest and largest divisions of the Internet. Many of these groups have a long history and cult following, and if you haven't used them before, get some background on Usenet groups before participating (see "Information Site 14," on page 89). As with basic email, the background you need for using Usenet is beyond the scope of this book. In this context, it's important to learn how Netscape can also be your interface to these amazingly open and often anarchic topical online discussion forums.

Netscape has a built-in newsreader that allows a user to read, subscribe, and post to Usenet groups through a separate window. The newsreader window will appear when you click on a link with a URL that points to a newsgroup (with the form "news:*newsgroupname*") or when you click on **Window | Netscape News** in the top menu bar. Like Netscape's email program, a useful feature of Netscape's newsreader is its ability to form a hyperlink that you can click on when a URL appears in a discussion group message. Netscape will fetch and display the file in the *Netscape Navigator* window as a single step. (For further documentation, see the pages on email and News in the Netscape online users' *Handbook*.)

6.3 Interactive Real-time Communications: From Talk to MUDs

Through a separate window during an Internet session, you can use a variety of other interactive and real-time multi-user communications programs. Many universities and corporations are using real-time interactive environments for instruction, information exchange, and real-time problem solving. (Many Net citizens, however, treat these communications links as endless and unproductive time sinkholes, so you've been warned.)

Multi-user environments use a special implementation of client–server software that allows real-time, synchronous communication over the Net. This usually involves a connection to a special port on a server that hosts the multi-user program.

The basic way of connecting to a multi-user communication server is to telnet to the server and then run the software on the remote system. (You need a telnet client to use this Internet

EMAIL AND USENET GUIDES

Name	URL
Guide to USENET at Indiana University	**http://scwww.ucs.indiana.edu/NetRsc/usenet.html**
EFF's Extended Guide to the Internet (choose email and Usenet from the contents)	**http://www.eff.org/papers/eegtti/eeg_toc.html**

connection; see section 7.3). The telnet link can be slow, and it is limited to the text-only VT–100 terminal features. A better way to connect is with a GUI client program that uses a graphical interface and contains features appropriate to the application (for access to software, see "Information Site 15," on page 91). You will always experience better results by using a client program designed for the specific communication environment rather than by using an ordinary telnet connection to the server.

Internet Talk: Real-time Communication for Two

The first real-time communications link on the Net was Internet Talk, in which two users link up and "talk" (i.e., type in text which is displayed on both users' screens) in real time. Talk splits the screen into two parts or windows, one for the local user, the other for the remote interlocutor, and what you type in your window gets displayed in real time in the corresponding window on the other user's screen. Talk requires the usual two-part client–server programs, often run from a shell account (the text-only command line mode on an Internet server) but also through a Windows program on a PC with a direct IP connection. Of course, Talk requires both users to be on the Net at the same time (that's what "real-time" means), so you need either to schedule a time or to find out if the person you want to "talk" to is online. To use Talk, you can fire up a telnet client helper application (see section 7.3) and login to a shell account if you have one, or use a Talk client in Windows.

Internet Relay Chat: The 24-hour Teleconference Line on the Net

Internet Relay Chat (IRC) is a multi-user real-time communications link that runs on several Internet servers around the world. IRC is like a virtual conference call using the Net's client–server architecture to connect your computer to an IRC server. IRC allows several channels for multiple simultaneous group discussions. When connected to an IRC server, you can chat with many people simultaneously and switch channels for other discussions with other groups. Chat allows one-on-one, many-to-many, and auditorium or one-to-many communications.

Netscape includes software, *Netscape Chat*, for connecting to an IRC server. This software works with *Netscape Navigator* 2.0

and above (Windows and Macintosh) and contains useful on-screen documentation and user aids for using IRC. *Netscape Chat* also works seamlessly with *Netscape Navigator* to allow users to send URLs in a Chat discussion so that the URLs appear as hyperlinks that can be clicked on and then viewed in Netscape.

MUD in Your Interface: Multi-User Virtual Reality Environments (MUDs, MOOs, MUSHes, MUSEs)

The Internet now contains many sites for interacting with other Net users in what are collectively known as MUSEs (Multi-User Environments) or MUSHes (Multi-User Shared Hallucinations/Multi-User Shells). These terms embrace a variety of programs running on various Internet servers that allow many people to login at the same time and engage in real-time role playing, game playing, dialogue, and information exchange. MUDs (Multi-User Dungeons/Multi-User Domains/Multi-User Dimensions) first emerged as virtual reality role-playing software for various kinds of games. MUDs are far beyond games in an ordinary sense now. In a MUD/MOO, users login, usually via telnet to a specific port on a server, assume a virtual identity, and interact with other identities. There are several good GUI MUD client programs that offer special features beyond ordinary telnet (see "Information Site 16," on page 92).

USING IRC WITH NETSCAPE

Topic	URL
Netscape Chat software for *Netscape Navigator*	**http://home.netscape.com/comprod/chat.html** **http://home.netscape.com/comprod/power_pack.html**
List of chat servers	**http://home.netscape.com/comprod/chat_svr.html**
IRC information, FAQs, and software	**http://www.kei.com/irc.html**

INFORMATION SITE 15

INFORMATION SITE 16

MULTI-USER ENVIRONMENTS

Name	URL	Comments
The MUD Resource Collection	**http://www.cis.upenn.edu/~lwl/mudinfo.html**	Links to MUD information sources.
Amberyl's Automated MUSH List	**http://www.cis.upenn.edu/~lwl/auto.html**	List of all MUDs and telnet addresses; find out where the MUDs are and which ones are up and running.
The MUD Connector	**http://www.absi.com/mud/mud.html**	Excellent total resource guide.
Educational Virtual Reality Page	**http://tecfa.unige.ch/edu-comp/WWW-VL/eduVR-page.html**	WWW Virtual Library resource page; excellent starting point.
Introduction to Educational Uses of MUDs	**http://www.itp.berkeley.edu/~thorne/MOO.html**	Good page of links to educational and social MUDs and MOOs.
Computer Writing and Research Labs (University of Texas at Austin), MUD and VR Research Page	**http://www.cwrl.utexas.edu/moo/index.html**	Good resource for educational uses of MUSE technology
Jennifer Smith's MUD FAQ with links to MUD client software	**http://math.okstate.edu/~jds/mudfaq-p2.html**	Get your MUD/MOO client programs here.
The Daedalus Group's Educational MOO Information Site (Austin, Texas)	**http://www.daedalus.com/net/border.html**	Information about and a list of educational MOO sites with telnet addresses.
The Mizzou MOO Page (University of Missouri)	**http://www.missouri.edu/~moo/**	Excellent resource for information on educational MOOs.

Although MUD originally designated a specific role-playing game (Multi-User Dungeon, an adventure game), MUD (now Multi-User Dimension) is now commonly used to designate the whole array of Multi-User environments, including MOOs (MUD Object Oriented), found on the Net. MOOs are created with a special programming language that allows the construction of an interactive virtual reality site complete with rooms, spaces, and objects that provide contexts and environments for users. There are some excellent MOO sites hosted by universities and research centers for creative interaction among people exploring a common subject or problem. There is also a new generation of MUDs emerging with graphical and Web interfaces. Watch for new developments in the software for implementing multi-user real-time environments.

Here are some pointers for learning more about MUSEs if you want to use and explore them further.

7
Extending the Interactive Multimedia Capabilities of the Web

The client–server structure of the Web allows users to interact with servers that can deliver files in any digital media format. Multimedia file formats, however, exist in many flavors—including some proprietary formats for specific software—and current Web clients like Netscape can't interpret, play, or display all of these formats. How then does the Web allow any kind of file to be delivered and used? Here's where Web client "helper applications" and "plug-ins" come in.

7.1 Multimedia Files and Web Client Helper Applications

A helper application (or "helper app" for short) is a separate program for viewing or playing a certain kind of file that Netscape has received over the Web but which Netscape itself cannot display. When Netscape receives a file format that it can't handle, it passes the file on to a helper app, which runs in a separate window on your screen. A "plug-in" application is similar in that it works in concert with Netscape to allow the playing or displaying of files that the client software does not support in itself, but the plug-in program works right in the Netscape window. (Sometimes these programs for handling multimedia files are called "viewers"; a "viewer" in this context means the same thing—a program that allows us to play or display a file that the Web client isn't programmed to handle by itself.)

When using helper apps or plug-ins with Netscape, the file name and file type is simply specified in the URL that you click on, and when the file is received by your computer, Netscape launches the program required for playing or displaying it. The idea is to create a seamless and nearly transparent way to use files in any media format on the Web.

For example, let's say you've clicked on a link to a video file. Two common formats for digital video are QuickTime and MPEG, and both types require a video helper app that Netscape can launch when the file comes in to your computer (see section 7.2 for software). When the video helper app is properly configured on your computer, the video file that you received from the Web will play in the helper application. You can then replay the file in the helper app, save it to your computer, or simply remove it by closing the program. You can also toggle between the Netscape and video helper app windows if you want to view other information while keeping the video file in the helper app. When you close or exit the helper app, you'll simply return to the Netscape window.

We've already covered another kind of helper application for using telnet with a Web client. Since telnet is not a file transfer protocol like Gopher, FTP, and HTTP, but a remote login protocol, your Web client passes on the telnet function to a separate telnet client program, which can be launched each time you use a URL containing the telnet protocol (like **telnet://locis.loc.gov**). (In Netscape, you set up a telnet client in the **Options** | **General Preferences** | **Apps** menu.)

USER NOTE
FILE FORMATS THAT NETSCAPE CAN DISPLAY OR PLAY

File Format	File Name Extensions	Displayed/Played As
HTML file	.html, .htm	Formatted text with hyperlinks and inserted inline images (if any)
Plain-text file	.txt, .text	Plain text
Audio files (with accompanying *NAplayer*)	.au, .aif, .aiff	Sound (requires sound card and speakers)
GIF image file	.gif	Inline image or separate image file
JPEG image file	.jpeg, .jpg	Inline image or separate image file
UNIX (x-bitmap) image file	.xbm	Usually inline image

7.2 Understanding Multimedia File Types on the Internet

The *Netscape Navigator* Web client brings files to your computer using various Internet protocols such as HTTP (Hypertext Transport Protocol, the Web server protocol), NNTP (Network News Transport Protocol), SMTP (Simple Mail Transport Protocol), Gopher, and FTP. Each protocol can support different file formats, that is, files containing different kinds of digital media. Netscape has the built-in capability to interpret and display on your computer several file formats. File types or formats are usually indicated by a file extension, which is the suffix after the dot in a file name (like "index.html," where .html is the file type).

Web servers and clients identify and manage file formats by using MIME, the Multipurpose Internet Mail Extension scheme. MIME specifications were initially developed to allow mixed media to be sent over the Internet as email, but for the Web this scheme provides the method for identifying the type of file and the media it contains. Web servers send MIME content–type information with the files that they deliver. Netscape and all other Web clients use the MIME scheme for identifying file formats and media types, a scheme that allows the incoming files to be interpreted and displayed by the Web client. Without this file identification system, your Web client wouldn't know how to differentiate text, audio, image, or video files and couldn't display and format them on your screen. Although there are other ways to tag or identify the bits that form a specific media type, the MIME scheme is the one used on the Net and by the apps that work with Net-delivered media.

7.3 Using and Configuring Multimedia Helper Applications

When Netscape retrieves a file with a format that Netscape itself cannot read and display, Netscape attempts to use an external helper application capable of reading the file. (These helper applications can be configured through the **Options | General Preferences | Helpers** menu.) There are helper applications for many kinds of files in all kinds of media.

To view or play video, sound, and proprietary media files, you need to install the appropriate program on your computer and

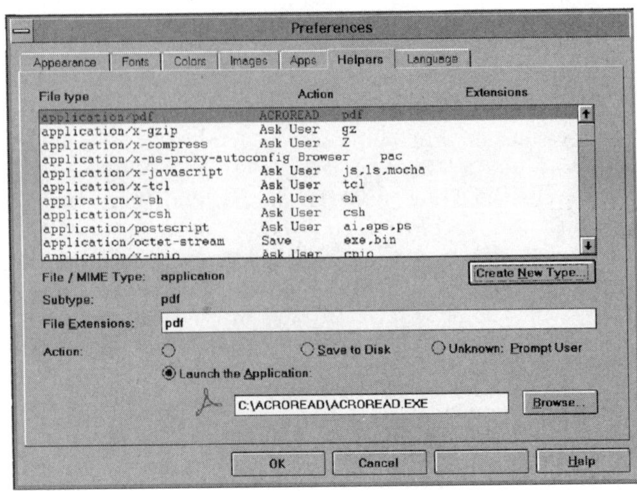

***Netscape Navigator* helper applications window.**

configure it for Netscape. Netscape's own online user's manual for helper apps and plug-ins will walk you through the process.

The multimedia capabilities of the Web are expanding in all directions, and it would be impossible to provide anything like a complete list of applications that can be used to play or display files delivered over the Web. Here are some common file formats and digital media used on the Web, and where you can

INFORMATION SITE 17

HELP AND RESOURCES FOR HELPER APPS AND PLUG-INS

Type	URL
Helper app installation	**http://home.netscape.com/assist/helper_apps/index.html**
Plug-in index and installation	**http://home.netscape.com/comprod/products/navigator/version_2.0/plugins/index.html**
Help and troubleshooting	**http://sunsite.unc.edu/louvre/about/tech.html**

get a copy of the program to use as a helper app or plug-in with Netscape and many other Web client programs.

Since new programs for Web-deliverable multimedia are always being developed, check the *Web Works* Website for links to up-to-date information and downloadable software. The following are reliable sites for information about multimedia helper apps for the Web.

7.4 Personal Agents

Personal or intelligent agents are programs that users can customize to perform independent tasks over the Web. Although not exactly a helper app, agents represent an advance in the use of the client–server architecture of the Web. Personal agents provide sophisticated clientside tools that can actually learn from your Web activities and help you find what you want, when you want it, or filter information so that you get exactly what you're looking for. Some agents perform customized searches, others perform tasks like link checking (are the links in your bookmarks file or another Web page still valid?) or site checking (has anything changed on Websites you are tracking or visit often?). New software for all kinds of Net tasks are emerging weekly, and I can only introduce the ideas that motivate their development and point out a few examples here. Unlike the largely freeware and shareware programs that connect thousands of users to the Net and Web, most agent software is being developed commercially as valued-added products.

For example, *Letizia*, an agent developed by Henry Lieberman at the MIT Media Lab, works in tandem with Netscape or Mosaic and "tracks the user's browsing behavior—following links, initiating searches, requests for help—and tries to anticipate what items may be of interest to the user. It uses a simple set of heuristics to model what the user's browsing behavior might be. Upon request, it can display a page containing its current recommendations, which the user can choose either to follow or to return to the conventional browsing activity."[1]

A useful and inexpensive Web agent or personal assistant is Quarterdeck Corporation's WebCompass. It performs customized searches of the Web in the background while you are doing

1. From **http://lieber.www.media.mit.edu/people/lieber/Lieberary/Letizia/Letizia.html**

INFORMATION SITE 18

HELPER APPS AND PLUG-INS FOR NETSCAPE AND *MOSAIC*

Media or File Format	Helper Application or Plug-in	Platforms	Download Source
Audio (Real Time)	Real Audio	Win; Mac	**http://www2.realaudio.com/release/download.html**
Audio Sound Files: .wav	**Win**: Media Player **Mac**: SoundApp	Win; Mac	Media Player comes with Windows 3.1x Mac: **http://wwwhost.ots.utexas.edu/mac/main.html**
Audio Sound Files: .au, .aif/aiff, .snd, .wav	**Win:** WHAM, Wplany **Mac:** .aiff and .snd capability built-in	Win; Mac	Win: **http://www.caboose.com/cwsapps/sound.html** Mac: **ftp://ftp.ncsa.uiuc.edu/Mosaic/Mac/Helpers/**
Video (Microsoft .AVI)	Video for Windows	Win	Win: **ftp://ftp.microsoft.com/Softlib/MSLFILES/wv1160.exe** Win: **http://www.caboose.com/cwsapps/video.html**
Video (MPEG)	**Win:** MPEGPlay (and other programs) **Mac:** Sparkle	Win; Mac	Win: **http://www.caboose.com/cwsapps/video.html** Win: **http://home.netscape.com/assist/helper_apps/** Mac: **ftp://ftp.ncsa.uiuc.edu/Mosaic/Mac/Helpers/**

Media or File Format	Helper Application or Plug-in	Platforms	Download Source
Video (quicktime movies)	Apple QuickTime Payer	Mac; Win 3.1x, Win 95, NT	**http://quicktime.apple.com/**
Adobe PDF (portable document format)	Adobe Acrobat Reader	Win; Mac; Unix	**http://www.adobe.com/acrobat**
Adobe PostScript Files	Aladdin Ghostscript Reader	Win; Mac; Unix	**http://www.cs.wisc.edu/~ghost/ghostscript/index.html**
Macromedia Shockwave (for Director)	Shockwave Viewer	Win; Mac	**http://www.macromedia.com/Tools/Shockwave/sdc/Plugin/index.htm**
SGML	SoftQuad Panorama	Win	Free version: **http://www.oclc.org:5046/oclc/research/panorama/panorama.html** Commercial: **http://www.sq.com/products/pst.htm**
Web programming:			
Java applets	Built-in Netscape 2.0 and higher	Win 95, NT; X-Win; Mac	Upgrade to Netscape 2.0 or above: **http://home.netscape.com/**

other work and creates a database of search results. This is one of the first examples of similar products now under development to make the Web easier to manage.

Netscape Corporation distributes a version of SmartMarks, a bookmarks managing program developed by First Floor software, that uses an agent program to monitor changes to Websites saved in your bookmarks file. It also allows customized searching of the Web by sending queries to multiple search engines while you do other work.

IBM has developed two intelligent agent products for new services, *infoMarket*, a clickable news ticker, and *InfoSage*, which

INFORMATION SITE 19

ACCESS TO HELPER APPS

Type	URL
Netscape's helper app lists (Win; Mac; Unix)	**http://home.netscape.com/assist/helper_apps/index.html**
NCSA's helper app lists (Win; Mac; Unix)	Win: **http://www.ncsa.uiuc.edu/SDG/Software/WinMosaic/viewers.htm** Mac: **http://www.ncsa.uiuc.edu/SDG/Software/MacMosaic/Supplementary/index.html** Unix: **http://www.ncsa.uiuc.edu/SDG/Software/XMosaic/faq-software.html**
Browsers, viewers, players (all platforms)	**http://groucho.gsfc.nasa.gov/Code_520/locator/brsrs.html**
Stroud's Consummate Winsock Apps List (Win)	**http://www.cwsapps.com** Mirror site: **http://www.caboose.com/cwsapps/cwsapps.html**
Mac Internet helpers directories	**http://www.wp.com/mwaters/machelp.html** **http://www.einet.net/tradewave/MacWeb/Machelpers.html** **http://wwwhost.ots.utexas.edu/mac/main.html**

can search and retrieve customized news information with user-defined content filters. There will be more products like these for searching and filtering information from the vast web of data on Net.

Agents such as these compensate for many of the shortcomings of online Web search engines, in that they can be customized to the individual user's needs and can perform more com-

PERSONAL INTELLIGENT AGENTS: SOFTWARE AND INFORMATION

Name	URL
Netscape, *SmartMarks*	**http://home.netscape.com/comprod/power_pack.html**
IBM, *infoMarket* news ticker and *InfoSage*	**http://www.infomkt.ibm.com/** **http://www.infosage.ibm.com/**
Quarterdeck Corporation, *WebCompass*	**http://www.quarterdeck.com/**
Rick Hauser (NetWatch), Top Ten Intelligent Agents/Information Agents	**http://www.pulver.com/netwatch/topten/tt9.htm**
The @gency, Serge Stinckwich's agent's page (best source of agent information on the web)	**http://www.info.unicaen.fr/~serge/sma.html**
MIT Media Lab Autonomous Agents Group	**http://agents.www.media.mit.edu/groups/agents/**
Pattie Maes (MIT), "Intelligent Software," *Scientific American* (1995)	**http://pattie.www.media.mit.edu/people/pattie/SciAm-95.html**
Henry Lieberman, *Letizia* Web agent project	**http://lieber.www.media.mit.edu/people/lieber/Lieberary/Letizia/Letizia.html**
Andy Wood, interface agents site	**http://www.cs.bham.ac.uk/~amw/agents/**

plex operations in the background while you do other computer work. Although this technology is still in its infancy, the great demand for more efficient ways to use the Web will push development forward very quickly.

7.5 Interactivity on the Web with Fill-in Forms

So far in this book we've been looking at all the intelligence built into Web client programs like Netscape for interacting with Web servers and displaying Web files. Much of the work of the Web is done clientside, and this makes for an efficient system. But there's also intelligence built into the Web on the server side, and this is what makes the Web a two-way, interactive media environment.

The Web is an interactive system through the use of fill-in forms that can send information back to a server. A Web form is an HTML file that has been encoded to create fields for user input—text fields, boxes or buttons to be selected, pull-down menus with options to be chosen. The interactivity works by allowing the user input in the form (from the clientside) to be sent to what is called a gateway interface (on the serverside), which allows the Web server to process information sent to it from a user. When a server receives data from a Web form, the server uses programs accessed through the Common Gateway Interface (CGI), an interface between the Web server software and other programs that interprets and processes the user input. If you've been using the Web for a while and have used a Web search engine, you're already familiar with a basic, but powerful, kind of interactive form—the search or query input to a CGI database program.

Forms and CGI programs can be used for many kinds of interactions with the remote computer—search a large database, subscribe to a commercial service, request information from a university or corporation, send an email message to an appropriate person in an organization, order a pizza with user-selected toppings and buy books or CDs. To insert your input and move around on a Web form, click on the text box or field you want to write in. You can also move from field to field with the **Tab** key. Use the mouse to click on boxes or radio buttons as well as the arrows on pull down menus. The Web form will have a **Submit** or **Send** button for sending the data to the server when you are finished filling in the form.

7.6 The Web and Deliverable Programming: Java Applets

The Web is now moving quickly into the next generation of networked computing with network-deliverable programming. Most of what we've been discussing so far concerns Web file *content* and how files are simply requested and displayed using all the various client–server protocols on the Net. Although hypertext and hypermedia make this basic client–server system very flexible and unlimited in range of content, the Web until recently limited clients to interpreting and displaying static content. What if we want to do more with the information? Process it clientside? Deliver and present more complex kinds of media, like 3-D modeling or virtual reality (VR), which require dynamic, user-interactive programming at the clientside?

The need for delivering programming along with content was solved by the Java programming language developed by Sun Microsystems. Netscape has formed a partnership with Sun's Java team to make *Netscape Navigator* a Java interpreter. The technical details of Java are beyond the scope of this book, but what Java does can be grasped readily by most Web users.

Java is a programming language that allows small programs called "applets" (mini-applications) to be used on the Internet with Web files. Java, like the Net, is hardware- and software-independent. This means that any Web server can deliver the applets and any Java-ready client can use them. Although there are some Java applets already being used on the Web, Java and

MORE ABOUT JAVA AND NETWORK-DELIVERABLE PROGRAMMING

Name	URL
Sun Microsystem's Java site	http://java.sun.com/
The W3 Consortium's Mobile Code Site (technical information)	http://www.w3.org/hypertext/WWW/MobileCode/
Netscape Navigator 2.0	http://home.netscape.com/comprod/products/navigator/version_2.0/index.html

INFORMATION SITE 21

Web-deliverable programming are still in the development stage. When fully implemented, Java will open up a whole new range of user-interactive, multimedia possibilities on the Net.

Netscape 2.0 and above for Unix, Windows 95, NT, and Mac is Java-capable. Expect more sophisticated versions of Netscape soon, and other Web clients will need to follow Netscape's lead.

8 Taking the Next Step: Becoming a Web Developer

The Web is different from all other communications media in that users can become producers. After you learn how to use the Web, you may soon begin wondering about how to create your own Web resources and connect your information to the Web. This book can't be your guide to developing and producing Web content, but it can prepare you with the right background so that you can take the next step. If you are interested in becoming a Web developer, here are some of the things you should consider before getting started, a list of what you'll need, and a directory of online guides that can teach you the specifics. As you might expect, most of the information you'll need for learning how to create Web files is on the Web.

8.1 Are You Ready to Become a Web Developer?

The Web is now the world's largest information resource, and its exponential growth will continue into the next decade. But the Web is already full of quickly produced, repetitive, and largely pointless files, much like the self-duplicating array of products in a shopping mall. So, before getting the required account on a Web server, remember that making a Web file available to the world has the same long-range effects as publishing in other media. You need to consider

- The overall image projected from the Web pages, how you want to represent yourself or your organization.
- The design and layout of the files.
- The kinds of links to supporting information, both on your own server and on other Websites.
- How to use multimedia effectively.

The Web is scalable in the sense that you can create and serve files at any level of complexity, from simple text files to sophisticated graphical and multimedia pages. Where you will begin on this sliding scale of complexity is usually a function of time, resources (human and financial), and technical ability.

Developing Web resources does require a substantial commitment of time, since you or your assistants will need to learn the basics of how the Web works, how HTML files function on the Web, how to create and organize HTML files, and how to create directories and install the files on a Web server. Furthermore, Web files, once they are made public, require a certain amount of maintenance. When you make files available on the Web, you are creating public access resources that Web users around the world will refer to as they add your URLs to their bookmarks files and create links to your files from their own HTML files. The metaphor of the web is appropriate, in that Web files interconnect to form an extremely elaborate and sophisticated pattern of cross-references and interrelations. If you move, remove, or fail to maintain your Web files, you tear a hole in the Web, and anyone who has created links to your materials will get error messages. Web information developers should be willing to make a commitment to provide a stable structure and long-term maintenance for their files.

8.2 What You Need to Begin

Space for Your Files on a Web Server

If you are using the Web on a LAN at your university or business, you may find that you already have access to directories on a server that will allow you to make materials available on the Web. Ask your local computer support person. If you are paying for Web access through an Internet Service Provider (ISP), you may have a certain amount of Web server space available as part of your monthly fee or for a nominal additional fee (see Chapter 3). Various ISPs have different procedures for requesting space on their Web servers. You should plan ahead and contact your provider or local computer support person in advance, since having access to the Web does not necessarily mean that you have space for your own files on a Web server, and you may need to fill out an application and wait for your request to be processed.

Basic Understanding of How to Work with Files on a Server

When you make files available on the Web, they need to be installed on a Web server (a server on the Net using HTTP). You will need an account on the server (password-protected access to an amount of disk space), and understanding of how to move your files to the server (generally via FTP), how to work with and organize your files when they are on the server (generally via telnet), and how to update your files when needed (generally by replacing an old file with a new version of the file). You may need software tools, such as FTP and telnet programs, to transfer your files from your own computer and to work with your files on the server. Most Web servers are UNIX machines, so Web development often requires learning some basic UNIX commands. Ask your computer support person for more information, and if you do need to know UNIX commands, refer to the UNIX guides listed in the Bibliography.

Basic Understanding of HTML

HTML is easy to learn, especially after you have a basic understanding of how the Web works. Anyone who has done word processing can learn HTML. One of the best texts that will help you start learning the basics of HTML is *A Beginner's Guide to HTML* **(http://www.ncsa.uiuc.edu/demoweb/html-primer.html)**. This hypertext document explains the basics of HTML in a straightforward way. You might want to print it out for future reference—simply use the **Print** option under the **File** menu in Netscape when you are viewing the *Beginner's Guide.*

HTML tags are simply ASCII (plain text) characters inserted into a text file to give various instructions to Web client programs. Because HTML files are ASCII files, they are platform-independent; and because they follow standard, consistent markup rules, they can be used by any Web client program. (There are some exceptions to this rule. Netscape and Microsoft have been experimenting with extensions to HTML standard markup; these extensions can be interpreted only by Web clients that know the additional tags).

In their most basic form, HTML tags start with a left angle bracket (<), then the name of the tag, and end with a right angle bracket (>). Tags are usually paired (for example, ⟨title⟩

and ⟨/title⟩). In the closing tag, a slash (/) precedes the name of the tag. Think of the beginning and ending tags as on and off switches for a certain kind of feature. More complicated tags will include additional information beyond simply the name of the tag within the angle brackets, such as instructions for defining alignment or spacing (see examples in the "User Notes" later in this chapter).

Once you understand the basics of HTML, you will find that it's easy to expand your knowledge by looking at the markup of others' Web files. When you see a file on the Web and you want to figure out what kind of markup the author used to create formatting, linking, and interactive features, use the **Document Source** option under the **View** menu in Netscape to display the HTML file. You can then toggle back and forth between the document source window that shows the HTML and the Netscape window that displays the file with all of its formatting and links, deciphering how the HTML markup is translated into various features by the Netscape client.

You can also download a Web file and work with it to see what changes as you edit the HTML markup. To download a file from the Web, use the **Save As** option under the **File** menu and save the file to a disk or your hard drive. You can then open the file in an HTML editing program (see "Information Site 23," on page 117), change the markup, and view your changes in Netscape. When you have downloaded a file from the Web, you are working with a local copy, and therefore, you cannot in any way harm or alter the "master" copy of the file on its Web server. Feel free to experiment and play with the file as you learn how it works and how to construct your own HTML markup. Remember, however, that if you use a significant portion of someone else's Web file to create your own, you must credit your source (see section 5.4).

The functions of HTML markup can be divided into four basic categories: markup that defines the structure of the HTML file and "meta-information" about the file, such as who created it; markup that gives Web client programs instructions for formatting the file on the screen; markup that creates links to other files or links within the file; and markup that defines interactive functionality, such as executing a script on a remote server.

MARKUP FOR THE STRUCTURE OF AN HTML FILE Every HTML file should have markup that identifies it as an HTML file and divides it into a "head" and a "body." The body of the file is what displays for the end user. The head is reserved for information about the file, such as its title, the name and email address of the person who created it, and the date when it was last revised. Although these elements in the head of the file are not necessary, they are very useful, not only for the end user, who might want to know how to contact the author or how recently the file has been updated, but also for the Web developer, who can use the markup in the heads of files to keep track of when the files have been updated and other relevant information.

USER NOTE
STRUCTURAL MARKUP AND META-INFORMATION

Tag	Explanation
⟨html⟩ . . . ⟨/html⟩	Identifies the beginning and end of the HTML file. These two markup elements should always be the first and last things you see in an HTML file.
⟨head⟩ . . . ⟨/head⟩	Distinguishes the head of the HTML file from the body; the head is where information about the file will be included. Information in the head is generally not visible to the end user unless he or she chooses to view the document source.
⟨title⟩ . . . ⟨/title⟩	Marks the title of the file; note that this is not the same as headings, which display in the body of the file. The title of a file is not visible when the page displays, but it is used in bookmarks files, search results, and other functions, so all HTML files should have a title included in the head.
⟨!--nondisplaying comments--⟩	Comment tags; this markup can be used to hide any text that you do not want to display. It is commonly used to identify the author of the file, his or her email address, notes on the revision history of the file, and other useful information that should be included in the head of the HTML file.
⟨body⟩ . . . ⟨/body⟩	The main body of the HTML file, which displays for the end user.

FORMATTING TAGS Web client programs display files only according to the way they are marked up in HTML, disregarding spaces, blank lines, or any other spatial arrangements that might display when you are viewing the ASCII file in a editing program. An ASCII file without any HTML markup will display as one long stream of text when a Web client program tries to present it as an HTML file. Therefore HTML markup is required for even the simplest spacial arrangements, such as line breaks and paragraph breaks. HTML markup provides only fairly crude formatting features in comparison to word processing programs and desktop publishing systems, but HTML is evolving quickly to meet the demand for more sophisticated formatting. The tags listed below represent only the most common, basic elements of HTML formatting.

CREATING LINKS TO OTHER FILES Although an HTML file is an ASCII file, it can include links to other types of files, such as image, sound, and video files. The HTML markup gives the Web

USER NOTE
BASIC FORMATTING TAGS

Tag	Explanation
⟨h1⟩ . . . ⟨/h1⟩	Heading level 1; this is the top level for headings and will display larger than other heading levels, 2 to 6. (Do not confuse this with the title, which is in the head of the document and does not display.)
⟨p⟩	Paragraph break. This tag breaks the current line and leaves a blank line before starting a new line of text.
⟨br⟩	Line break. This tag breaks the current line and starts a new line of text directly under it.
⟨hr⟩	Horizontal rule. This tag inserts a line across the page.
⟨ul⟩ ⟨li⟩ ⟨li⟩ ⟨/ul⟩	Unordered (unnumbered) list. The ⟨ul⟩ tags begin and end the list, and the ⟨li⟩ tags identify each list item. A list can have any number of items, and you can embed or nest lists within lists. (An ordered, or numbered, list uses the tags ⟨ol⟩ and ⟨/ol⟩; list items in an ordered list are automatically numbered.)

client program instructions for retrieving and displaying or playing other files that work in conjunction with the HTML file itself. For example, the HTML markup will tell the Web client program how to format the text of the HTML file and will also tell it how to retrieve an image file and include the image in a certain position in the display. These types of links to other files will be executed without the user's interaction. Other links to files outside the one being displayed are offered to the user as hotlinks, and clicking on these links will bring other files to the Web client for display. Similarly, the user can click on hotlinks that will jump to other sections of the same HTML file.

MARKUP FOR INTERACTIVITY HTML markup provides instructions not only for local features, such as formatting and creating hypertext links, but also for remote interactivity with a server on the Internet. For example, when you click on an image and receive a file that corresponds to the specific area of the image, you are using what's called a sensitive image map (ISMAP) that

Tag	Explanation
⟨dl⟩ ⟨dt⟩ ⟨dd⟩ ⟨dt⟩ ⟨dd⟩ ⟨/dl⟩	Definition list. The ⟨dl⟩ tags begin and end the list. Each ⟨dt⟩ identifies a new definition term, which will be displayed flush left, and each ⟨dd⟩ provides the definition for that term, which will be indented five spaces under the ⟨dt⟩ line. A definition list can have any number of definition terms and definitions under those terms. Lists can be embedded within lists.
⟨pre⟩ . . . ⟨/pre⟩	Preformatted. Used to maintain the spacing or layout of a file or section of a file as it is displayed in ASCII.
⟨i⟩ . . . ⟨/i⟩	Italicize. The text within the tags will display in italics.
⟨b⟩ . . . ⟨/b⟩	Bold. The text within the tags will display in boldface.
⟨img src= . . . ⟩	Insert an inline image. Tag means "image source." See "HTML Links to Other Files," on page 114.

determines what file to send based on the coordinates of the exact point where you clicked with your mouse. And whenever you use any type of form on the Web, you are actually executing a "script" (a file containing line-by-line commands to perform some function) or a separate program on the remote server. HTML markup for forms allows all kinds of interaction with users, but the creation of the form in an HTML file also requires a matching script or program on the server (see section 7). These scripts often run in the cgi-bin directory on the Web server, so whenever you see markup that includes "cgi-bin," you can generally assume that the markup is referring to a script on the server that will perform some action for you.

As the demand for Web interactivity grows, expect to see more and more complicated markup that will provide the user with options such as requesting specific information from a remote database, executing 3-D modeling and full motion animation, and generating data and/or Web files "on the fly." HTML markup that provides options for interactivity transforms your Web client into a gateway to computing power, programs, and databases on servers around the world. After learning basic HTML, there are really no limits to what Web users can learn in order to be creative Web producers and publishers.

USER NOTE
HTML LINKS TO OTHER FILES

Tag	Explanation
⟨img src="*imagename*.gif"⟩	Link to an image that will be displayed with the text of the HTML file (also called an inline image).
⟨a href="http://*hostname.domain/directory-path/filename*.html"⟩ . . . ⟨/a⟩	Link to another HTML file. The "a" identifies the anchor, marking the text that will display as a link, and "href" is a hypertext reference to the other file, specified here by the URL in quotation marks.
⟨a href="#section"⟩ . . . ⟨/a⟩ ⟨a name="section"⟩ . . . ⟨/a⟩	Link to another section in the same file. The "name" tag identifies the point in the file to jump to from the "href" link.

8.3 Software Tools for Creating and Editing HTML Files

HTML files are ASCII (plain text) files, so technically you can create Web files in any word processing program by typing in the markup and saving the file as an ASCII file. Practically speaking, however, it's best to take advantage of one of many software tools that are specifically designed for creating and editing HTML files. These programs are generally known as HTML editors or Web authoring software, and fall into three basic categories: add-ons to word processing and desktop publishing programs, stand-alone HTML editing programs, and HTML editing–Web development software that works in conjunction with a Web server.

Add-ons to Word Processing and Desktop Publishing Programs

Most major word processing and desktop publishing programs now have add-ons or even built-in features that allow you to use the program you're already accustomed to, such as *WordPerfect*, *Word*, or *PageMaker*, to create Web files. The *Word Internet Assistant*, for example, will allow you simply to save the *Word* file you're working on as an HTML file. The program compares the *Word* proprietary formatting of the file with similar features in HTML markup and does a rough conversion, sub-

TUTORIALS FOR LEARNING HTML

Site	URL	Comments
Daedalus's Guide to the Web: HTML Guides	**http://www.georgetown.edu/labyrinth/general/hypertext.html**	Useful index with links to the best online HTML guides.
Thomas Boutell's Web FAQ	**http://www.boutell.com/faq/**	An excellent set of answers to "Frequently Asked Questions," including HTML authoring.
Web Developer's Virtual Library	**http://WWW.Stars.com/**	All the Web tools conveniently indexed.

INFORMATION SITE 22

stituting HTML markup for the *Word* formatting and omitting any formatting that doesn't have an exact HTML equivalent.

The advantages of such programs are that they are relatively easy to use, especially if you already know how to use the other features of the word processing program, and you don't need to see or understand the HTML markup, since the program simply does it for you. The latter point, however, is also a disadvantage, in that if you don't understand the HTML markup, you can't make knowledgeable choices about how to change the markup if you don't like the program's automatic conversion. And since the page layout and design afforded by HTML is a great deal less sophisticated than that of word processors, you will generally want to make changes in the way the program has "dumbed down" the original layout. Generally you will find that these add-ons are best for an initial rough conversion of a word-processed file, and then you will often want to tailor and adjust the resulting HTML file using a stand-alone HTML editing program.

Stand-alone HTML Editing or Authoring Programs

A great variety of HTML editing programs have been developed recently, and you shouldn't have any trouble finding one to suit your needs for your operating system. These stand-alone, independent programs are useful both for creating HTML files from scratch and for editing existing files, including those generated by other programs, such as word processors. These programs provide menus and buttons for inserting markup so that you can easily change the look and functionality of your HTML files. Some HTML editing programs hide the markup, so that what you see on the screen is the same as how the file will display in a Web client program (WYSIWYG, or "what you see is what you get"), but most will display the markup for you. This option is very useful, once you get used to reading HTML markup, because it allows you to see how the file is constructed; this ability makes it much easier to correct problems and experiment with the markup to get exactly the effects you want.

When you choose an HTML editing program, check to see what version of HTML markup it's designed to use. HTML 2.0 has been the basic standard, and programs like *HTML Writer* will give you all the buttons and menus you need for getting started with this standard, but none of the more sophisticated features of HTML 3.0 or Netscape Extensions (like tables, centering, backgrounds, and frames). *HTML Writer* is a very good beginners' tool because it is extremely easy to understand, but once you get into more sophisticated markup, you would need to type in by hand anything beyond HTML 2.0. Other useful programs, such as the *Hot Dog* editor, are designed with buttons and menus for HTML 3.0 markup, making them more complicated but also more sophisticated HTML editing programs.

Web Client–Server Editing Programs

The most sophisticated HTML editing programs are those that include options for creating scripts and other supplements to the HTML markup. These programs are designed with the assumption that the features you will want to include in your Web resources, such as interactivity, require scripts and programs that will run on the Web server. For example, you might want to create a Web file that includes forms that allow a user to type in queries that are sent to the Web server, which interacts with a database and returns the information to the user. With interactive forms, you could type in your stock ticker

HTML EDITORS

Site	URL
Web Authoring Tools List (W3 Consortium)	**http://www.w3.org/hypertext/WWW/Tools/**
Tom Magliery's List of HTML Editors (University of Illinois)	**http://union.ncsa.uiuc.edu/HyperNews/get/www/html/editors.html**
Stroud's Reviewed List of Windows HTML Editors	**http://www.cwsapps.com/html.html**
Microsoft *Word Internet Assistant*	**http://www.microsoft.com/msword/fs_wd.html**
HTML Writer	**http://lal.cs.byu.edu/people/nosack/**
Hot Dog HTML Editor	**http://www.sausage.com/**
Netscape Gold	**http://home.netscape.com/comprod/products/navigator/gold/index.html**
Web Weaver for Macintosh	**http://www.northnet.org/best/**

INFORMATION SITE 23

numbers and get the most recent quotes. Or type in your name and ID number and check your grades from last semester. The possibilities for Web client-server interactivity are unlimited (see Chapter 7).

Netscape *Gold* is a Web authoring package that allows you to view and edit your files locally and then upload your edited files to your Web server (via FTP to your own directories). Netscape *Gold* is a WYSIWYG editor: the HTML markup is not displayed, but inline images and the effects of the point and click HTML features are. (The inability to see the tags or make changes easily to existing markup is one deficiency of this editing package, however.) The ease of editing, viewing, and uploading files back to the server within one program is an attractive feature. Products like this will make Web developing even easier and more accessible to many users.

9 Web Philosophy 101: Cyberknowledge for the Networked Age

This chapter is intended to introduce questions, bend paradigms, and provoke thought about some of key ideas that drive the Web in its social context. The issues and ideas presented here are parts of an ongoing process of thought, not a manifesto or completed argument. New web filaments drawn from these topics will be presented and updated on the *Web Works* Website.

We come full circle from the approach introduced at the beginning of this book: the Web's user-centered hypermedia form leads to more user participation and intervention in the course of ideas that motivate and follow the technology. Models for thinking about networked digital culture are necessarily paradigms in motion. In the Web environment, you can't step into the same datastream even once.

9.1 Net Effects: The Revolution Is Being Digitized

The Web is a global, dynamic, multimedia communications environment, not simply a new medium. Calling the Web a new medium implies extension, comparison, or continuity with prior or existing media technology. The Web's interactive, hypermedia user interface (on the client side) and globally distributed content and delivery system (on the server side) make it an info-environment, something more inhabited than used. It presents us with a completely new way of thinking about communications, media, and information.

For the first time in history, we are witnessing a communications revolution that will be complete in one generation. Many inventors of communications media—the early Christian developers of the codex manuscript, Gutenberg and moveable type, Alexander Graham Bell and telephony—did not live to see the far-reaching social effects of their technologies. It took several centuries for the codex manuscript to configure social institutions like schools, libraries, and law courts, and several more for the printed book to reconfigure the old institutions and help produce the era of the nation-state, the middle class, a mass reading public, and modern individualism. It took many generations for the telephone to have the near-transparent universality it has today, and two generations for television to reach its present level of social saturation. Professors in their forties, who grew up learning to take TV for granted, now regularly feel alienated from their students, who take using the Net and Web for granted. Many undergrads at colleges and universities across North America use email as easily and regularly as their professors use the telephone.

Furthermore, developers of media technology can never predict or foresee the outcomes and consequences of the technology. Gutenberg thought he was providing a way to make better and more easily reproduced manuscripts. Bell thought he was creating an instrument to aid the deaf. We have not yet witnessed the full global effects of the Internet and World Wide Web, but they will be far beyond what we think about them at the moment.

The Web also allows consumers and users of information to become producers and developers of new content. The traditional divide between producer and consumer is being eroded; authority and control over information is now being dispersed to millions of people across the globe. The interactive nature of the Web and hypermedia also restructures the sites of authority and knowledge in Net culture. Networked hypermedia users are free to create their own webs of information and knowledge, not as passive consumers but as active agents in their own use of the media.

9.2 The Medium Is the Message Revisited: The Net and Web as a Self-disclosing System

The Net and Web are different from all prior communications media in that information about how the technology works is built into the system itself. The most up-to-date information about the Net—its history, design, growth, and most of all, user access—is always on the Net itself. No other communications medium even approximates this.

Marshall McLuhan noted that the content of any new medium is an immediately prior medium: printed books at first reproduced the content and look of manuscripts, television at first reproduced the content of radio programs and live theater. But he never foresaw the Web: part of the content of the Web is the Web itself. It's the world's first self-documenting or self-disclosing medium.

No other communications technology has ever been developed in which all users have access to a body of information about the technology transmitted in very medium of communication used by the technology. This feature is in part a result of the Internet as an open system and as a client–server, user-interactive system. Web users readily and easily become Web producers. Contrast this state of affairs with radio, TV, or telephone: none of these technologies document themselves with information about the technology in the medium used by the technology. You can't learn how a TV works or how TV broadcast technology works by using a TV. You certainly can't become—or even learn how to become—a TV broadcaster and develop programming yourself simply because you have a TV and an antenna or cable hookup. The Web turns everything we thought we knew about communications technology inside out; it radically reconfigures our experience of knowledge, information, and communication.

9.3 Dynamic Not Static, or the Moving Target

Imagine a library in which all the books and periodicals were cross-referenced, and any page contained references to all other pages of related information. Imagine that this library had thousands of assistants that could fetch you the cross-referenced information in any other document any time you wished. Imagine that you could assemble the information sources in any way you wished and that you could add your own annotations and commentary. Imagine that this library is constantly growing with no central librarian in charge, and that readers, writers, and publishers don't want any one person in charge.

Imagine that this library grew to be able to cross-reference and cross-index all recorded information in any medium. And imagine that the library developed a way to re-index and re-catalog itself continuously.

Now imagine that the library contained books and media whose authors or producers constantly changed and updated the contents. Imagine that the very nature of this library precludes static or fixed records of any kind.

Imagine next what would happen if any of the blocks of information were changed or updated without the whole library adjusting to the new or changed contents.

9.4 Borges and the Library Labyrinth

In Jorge Luis Borges's wonderfully playful and prescient story "The Library of Babel," the narrator imagines an infinite library that contains all the world's knowledge, past, present, and future, in all languages. This vast library also contains a true catalog of itself, thousands of false catalogs, and refutations of the true and false catalogs. While all copies of books in the infinite library are unique, there are many inexact duplicates and facsimiles, varying in nearly undetectable changes or omissions (a letter here, a comma there). To find a way in this info-universe, everyone searches for the master librarian, who is like a god, knowing all the books and their locations. The narrator imagines a library that is unlimited and cyclical, repeating itself in its own disorder.[1]

We can read this story as a parable of the Internet. The Net and Web contain their own catalogs and commentaries, true and false, and the Web is quite amazingly self-documenting. Once we are taken in by the power of our digital library, we imagine it to contain all there is; knowledge and experience outside the digital domain of the Net becomes inaccessible, unrepresented, out of the loop. But the Web is still far from containing the sum total of human knowledge. It's an endless labyrinth construction site where everyone entering becomes a cyber-Ariadne, attempting to thread an ever-expanding digital maze.

9.5 Limitations and Challenges of Web Technology

Net and Web technology have developed more quickly than any earlier medium, and this speed of development has a social impact all its own. There are human limitations with any technology, but even though the Wright brothers couldn't have

1. Jorge Luis Borges, *Labyrinths* (New York: New Directions, 1962), 51–58.

imagined the NASA space shuttle, the shuttle wouldn't be possible without the first flight. It will take a while before the broad social, political, and economic implications of the Net and Web are understood. The following are a few points to consider as we live in the new information environment of the Web.

1. *Data is not knowledge.* Multiplication of data and ease of access to information do not produce knowledge or understanding. But neither do large libraries or archives. Rational human agency is required to convert data and information into knowledge.

2. *The lateral or horizontal distribution of information is increasing more quickly than rational organization or coherence.* The Web and Net provide nonhierarchical associations and connections among various kinds of content in various media. This is the liberating force of hypertext and hypermedia. But the Web's decentralization and nonhierarchical structure may create an illusion of equivalence among sources of content, flattening or leveling their perceived value. Evaluation and interpretation remain the highest powers of thought for using digital media and data.

3. *How do we deal with the dynamic, not static, nature of the Web as a system when we need reliable access to information?* The nature of the Web is change; it is rewritten and rewoven daily, hourly. Linkrot is inevitable. The Internet started as an invention to allow a network to work even when sections of it were unreliable. Internet technology itself is reliable (most of the time), but the fast proliferation of the Web has created unreliable information connections when files are moved, changed, or renamed. Servers can be down or taken off the Net. The URL thus has an inherent weakness as a "resource locator" since it points only to a place on a server where a file resides, not to an actual document like an ISBN or even a Library of Congress call number. One solution: the Internet Society and the W3 Consortium are looking at ways of implementing a "Universal Resource Number" that would identify files and documents no matter where they were served or what directory path they were on.[2]

Some of these limitations can be overcome and corrected by more intelligence being supplied at the user and client sides of the Web—better search engines and indexing software, smarter personal agents to do customized searches and organize infor-

2. See **http://www.w3.org/pub/WWW/Addressing/Addressing.html**

mation—but more needs to be done at the distribution points, at Websites that design the hypermedia resources and provide useful and connected paths of information for users.

9.6 Hypertext, Hypermedia, Theory

Much valuable theory and models for implementation have been written for hypertext and hypermedia since Ted Nelson's *Literary Machines* and the idea for the Xanadu project.[3] The great promise of hypertext and hypermedia as a way of reconfiguring knowledge, authority, authorship, and the role of the reader is still to be realized, and the Web has provided a way to implement hypertext principles in ways unforseen by early pioneers of the idea.

All hypertext/hypermedia file arrays, however, are inevitably bound and conflicted by two limitations: the essentially finite or closed system of even the richest collection of data files and the necessary element of human agency on both the authoring and user ends. Hypermedia doesn't just happen; it requires producers. Much has been written and theorized about the liberating effects of hypertext/hypermedia on readers and writers; but the power of this liberation will be always bounded by the human-authored finite limits of the content array. The Web, with its openness and dynamic form, allows one possible way to work around the limits of hypermedia when modeled on a static array of content. If the data array is constantly changing and growing from multiple distribution and production points, a hypermedia user can constantly update the web of information needed. The Web has limits, but the state of the possible content array is not one of them.

What are we doing when we create a hypertext document array and when view hypermedia with a client program on the Web? Are hypertext/hypermedia files—commonly called "documents" or "pages"—simply maps of existing knowledge connections or new, productive representations of knowledge? Are they descriptions of possible connections, affiliations, parallels,

3. The literature on hypermedia, both in print and on the Net, proliferates like the Web itself. For background in print, see Theodor H. Nelson, *Literary Machines* (Swarthmore, Pa.: Author, 1981); Paul Delany and George P. Landow, eds., *Hypermedia and Literary Studies* (Cambridge, Mass.: MIT Press, 1991); George P. Landow, *Hypertext: The Convergence of Contemporary Critical Theory and Technology* (Baltimore: Johns Hopkins University Press, 1992); and George P. Landow, ed., *Hyper/Text/Theory* (Baltimore: Johns Hopkins University Press, 1994).

or substitutions or a newly created implementation of them? That we still talk in terms of book images for the Web ("pages," "documents," and "files"), rather than in terms indicating the removal of physical media limits (something like "fields," "arrays," or "webs"), reveals a transitional phase in digital networked culture.

A new multimedia configuration, however, is more than the sum of its parts. An integrated set of hypermedia documents creates new paths of conceiving and foregrounds the necessity of thinking in relational terms. Hypertext/hypermedia can unfold what was there all the time—interconnections in language, thought, and representation—but unrepresentable in the static unilinearity of print and the physical information units of text.

Hypertext is structurally parallel to the figure of metonymy, not metaphor: hypertext presents horizontal substitutions, equivalences, increments, not new fusions of terms and concepts. It is parataxis, coordination, setting things in order side by side, not hypertaxis, rational ordering, ranking, prioritizing, subordinating. Hypertext says "and, but, or, on the other hand, and, and . . . " not "since, because, although, either . . . or, neither . . . nor. . . ."

Hypertext and hypermedia poorly replicate standard categories of authorship. Hypertext documents can have multiple writers or authors, but they also link texts from multiple authors. Hypertext documents often obscure and even erase traditional authorship. Hypertexts are strangely parallel to the traditional texts of preprint culture in that multiple authorship and dynamic change are expected and inherent in the genre. It is often as meaningless to ask who the author is of *Beowulf* or Genesis as it is to ask who the author is of a Website.

Though not susceptible to authorship in the traditional sense, hypertext documents assume human agency, a productive agency. (Noting that some hypertext documents and files are poorly implemented or fail to exploit the different kind of representation in hypertext is a comment on the abilities of the agents behind the files, not a comment on the medium or the technology.) The term "agent" is thus a better term for the author(s) or originator(s) of networked hypertext.

9.7 New Communities on the Net

I think a word about the communities of people that the Net and Web have helped create should be included here. I've been a Net user for seven years and have watched the Net and its users go through several life cycles, from the early "wow" stage and an ethic of elite insiders to a sense of both local and global citizenship. The Net is no utopia, nor will it produce one, but it has introduced a new possibility into the world, and as the technology becomes cheaper and even more globally available, it will continue to reconfigure how we think about our lives as members of multiple communities.[4]

For the most part, the Net follows or incorporates ordinary social configurations—by gender, race, class, and nationality—but some striking new configurations and counter-configurations have emerged that should not be ignored or discounted. The Net is the only system of human relations I know of that is basically anarchic and nonhierarchical. There are no laws except those consented to by users, no police force, no central administration imposing rules. Governments and commercial communications providers have attempted to intervene in Net society, but usually with insignificant and embarrassing results. It's common knowledge that not all people have the same access to computers or the Net, but no one is excluded from the Net or Web on the basis of race, class, sex, religion, or physical handicap.

Access to the Net, of course, is easier to remedy than self-exclusion or technophobia, which, alas, often cut along race, gender, and class lines. Entry-level hardware for using the Net is no more expensive than a TV and cable access, and many working-class families in North America pay far more for cable TV access than they would for unlimited Net access.

The growth of the Internet in the 1990s has been extraordinary. Connectivity is growing in developing nations around the world, bringing about a new transnational configuration of information, communication, and business. Governments have yet to deal with this fact, but many corporations have and are paving the way for whatever comes next for the Net.

9.8 Netizens: The Real Internet Society

The openness of the Net can be abused (and it has been—everyone knows the stories), and the Net can simply reproduce in another form all the disparities and banal nastiness that are

4. See Howard Rheingold's now-classic account of vitual communities, based on his experiences on The WELL: *The Virtual Community: Homesteading on the Electronic Frontier* (New York: HarperCollins, 1994). See Rheingold's Web site for electronic supplements: **http://www.well.com/user/hlr/**

part of the noncomputerized human condition. But what is so surprising, astonishing, really, is that the Net generally works to everyone's benefit.

On the whole, Net citizens usually help other citizens, provide useful information when asked for, and respect differences in the global electronic community. The vast majority of Net citizens are also on their guard against misuse of the open system, personal abuse, or exploitation, but generally enjoy debate and even heated disagreement. The Net and Web allow everyone with access to argue a point of view or promote a cause, develop a creative array of multimedia materials, and distribute information in an easily usable form. To become a new user of the Net and Web is to become a member of an open society, a citizen in local and global communities. Intellectual property is to be respected, though not to the extremes that the commercial copyright industries would like to see imposed strictly to enhance profits. Fair use does not impede marketability.

9.9 Practicing Net Citizenship

Many Net citizens want to be more than channel surfers and passive consumers. There are major issues to be resolved with far-reaching implications at all social levels—free speech rights on the Net, the rapid commercialization of Net technology and an inadequate payback structure for educational and research institutions who developed the technology, democratic access, intellectual property and copyright in the digital age, continued deregulation and competition of telecom industries nationally and globally, to name only a few. Ignorance is not bliss for the Net.

Recent U.S. legislation and political debate reveals that there are some misguided governmental and commercial forces at work that would restrict the use and exchange of information and police communications in ways unknown or inconceivable to the Net today. Net and Web users, therefore, also need to be social advocates who can intervene in local and national policy debates. While you become familiar with the resources of the Web, please take time to stay informed about the issues that affect Web users and Net citizens. If we want an open and widely accessible Net, we need to be willing to take our citizenship seriously enough to insist on having a voice in policy and the future of communications technologies.

A good way to begin taking Net citizenship seriously is to become familiar with the information and statement of issues on the Electronic Frontier Foundation's Website **(http://www.eff.org/)**. You may also want to join EFF or a similar organization. The EFF states its purpose as follows.

> Every day decisions are being made that will affect your life online. Decisions about what sorts of technology you can use to protect the privacy of your communications. Decisions about what services you will be able to get over the emerging national information infrastructure. Decisions that are made before you even know that there are choices. The Electronic Frontier Foundation has been working since July 1990 to ensure that the civil liberties guaranteed in the Constitution and the Bill of Rights are applied to new communications technologies. Our members join EFF to make sure that they are informed about the issues and debates that will shape the future of electronic communications **(http://www.eff.org/EFFdocs/join_eff.html).**

INFORMATION SITE 24

HYPERMEDIA THEORY AND CYBERKNOWLEDGE ISSUES

Site	URL	Comments
Online readings for Technology and the Humanities	**http://www.village.virginia.edu/readings/**	From the Institute for Advanced Technology in the Humanities, University of Virginia.
William Mitchell's *City of Bits* site	**http://www-mitpress.mit.edu/City_of_Bits/**	Excellent browsing point for issues discussed in this MIT professor's book; go to **Surf Sites**.
Wired magazine / *Hotwired*	**http://www.hotwired.com/**	The cybertimes; archives of articles, multimedia happenings.
The Xanadu project's FAQ	**http://www.aus.xanadu.com/xanadu/faq.html**	The theory for Ted Nelson's Xanadu proposal.
Jerome McGann's, "The Rationale of Hypertext"	**http://www.village.virginia.edu/public/jjm2f/rationale.html**	One of the best discussions of the implications of hypertext.

EFF also maintains an excellent set of lists for international, national, and state governments **(http://www.eff.org/govt.html)** and archives of policy information. The Center for Democracy and Technology fulfills a similar mission **(http://www.cdt.org/)**.

The best Website for keeping informed about government policy issues and bills as they work through the U.S. Congress is the "Thomas" site at the Library of Congress **(http://thomas.loc.gov/)**. From here you can search a database of all bills pending in the House and Senate and the full text of the *Congressional Record*. All branches of government have only just begun to deal with the new issues in telecommunications, technology policy, intellectual property, and civil rights in the networked and digital media age. LC-Thomas will remain a primary source for up-to-the-minute information on key issues that will affect all of us.

Site	URL	Comments
Computer Mediated Communication magazine	**http://www.december.com/cmc/mag/current/toc.html**	Excellent online journal edited by John December.
Journal of Post-Modern Culture	**http://jefferson.village.Virginia.edu/pmc/**	Many articles discuss issues in electronic culture.
Mark Poster's Courses at UC-Irvine	**http://www.hnet.uci.edu/mposter/index.html**	Innovative courses by the author of *The Second Media Age*.
Postmodern Theory, Culture Studies and Hypertext	**http://www.academic.marist.edu/1/culture.htm**	Excellent access point to online resources.
Journals and Zines on the Web	**http://humanitas.ucsb.edu/shuttle/journals.html**	A "Voice of the Shuttle" page; excellent, reliable site.
Cyberculture, Culture and Technology Resources	**http://humanitas.ucsb.edu/shuttle/science.html**	A "Voice of the Shuttle" page; excellent, reliable site.

For access to political information about the Net, see also the Harvard Kennedy School of Government's Online Political Information Network, which maintains links to resources on the politics of the Net and the NII **(http://ksgwww.harvard.edu/~ksgpress/pol-net.htm)**.

9.10 Thinking with the Web

The *Web Works* Website will continue to be a resource for using the Web itself as an instrument for thought, criticism, and analysis of digital and networked culture. In "Information Site 24" (pp. 128–29) and "Information Site 25" (below) you will find some important starting points for thinking through, and with, the Web.

INFORMATION SITE 25

NETIZENS' ISSUES

Name	URL
Electronic Frontier Foundation (EFF)	**http://www.eff.org/**
Center for Democracy and Technology	**http://www.cdt.org/**
Howard Rheingold's page at The WELL	**http://www.well.com/user/hlr/**
Computer Professionals for Social Responsibility (CPSR)	**http://snyside.sunnyside.com/home/**
Library of Congress, Thomas	**http://thomas.loc.gov/**
Kennedy School of Government, Online Political Information Network	**http://ksgwww.harvard.edu/~ksgpress/opinhome.htm**

Glossary

account. Protected user access to a networked computer through a unique username and password. When an account is set up for you on a computer system—for example, a **LAN***, a corporate computer, or an **Internet host** or **server**—a systems administrator assigns you a username (**login** name) and a password for access to the computer and a certain amount of disk space. With the user account comes access to computer resources like programs or Internet access.

agent. An autonomous program, similar to a **robot**, that works on behalf of a user to perform a user-defined computing task, like searching for specific information or comparing data from different sources.

analog. In computing and electronics, analog refers to a signal that is continuously varying throughout an unlimited range of values (soft, loud amplitude; high, low frequency or pitch; strong, weak in amount of signal). Signals commonly found in "nature" are all analog (for example, voice, sounds, temperature), as are humanly produced electromagnetic signals (such as, light, telephone, radio, TV). See **digital**.

anchor. The place in a **hypertext** document that provides a link to another file. Anchors are created by **HTML** tags that define the kind of hyperlink.

anonymous FTP. An open-access way of using **FTP** for **downloading** files from a server that you don't have an **account** on. Most Net and Web software is now configured to perform an "anonymous login" automatically when you click on a **hypertext** link to a file on an FTP **server**, or download a file with an FTP graphical interface program.

applet. A small computer **application** (program). A program that can be transferred over a computer network and run on a user's computer with appropriate software. Sun Microsystem's Java programming language allows applets to be delivered on the Web and run in a user's Web **client** or in software configured to work with the Web client.

application (app). Any computer program that performs a certain function, but distinct from the **operating system** that allows the program to run. A specific word processing program is an app that will run on a computer. *Netscape Navigator*, technically speaking, is a **World Wide Web client** program or application, written for various platforms and operating systems.

*Text in boldface indicates cross-referenced terms.

archie. An Internet "archi(v)e" tool or indexing system for locating files on anonymous **FTP** servers. Users access the index by making search requests of an Archie **server**. One of the first indexing and search tools used on the Internet.

ASCII. American Standard Code for Information Interchange; a standard format for representing typographical symbols in the **bytes** used by computers. This standard makes it possible for computers to share and exchange text data. An ASCII file usually means a plain-text file, a file containing the main characters of a keyboard with no additional (hidden) computer code. Basic ASCII, of course, is extremely limited as way of representing languages, since it assumes English and the Roman alphabet.

asynchronous. Not at the same time or not dependent on something happening at the same time. Email, fax, and voice mail are forms of asynchronous communication. See **synchronous**.

backbone. The high-speed data lines and **routers** that connect main computers or other networks. In the United States, the main **Internet** backbone was initially developed and maintained by the National Science Foundation, but since 1995 it is developed and maintained by major telecommunications companies. The high-speed data lines connecting university and regional networks are also commonly called backbones.

bandwidth. The speed at which data can be transmitted and presented, usually measured in **bits** per second. The bandwidth you have available is a function of physical hardware connections (**modems**) plus the data speed of the main network line that your computer is connected to. If you've got a fiber-optic high-speed data backbone running through your local network, your bandwidth will be greater than what's possible with a computer and a modem on an ordinary phone line. "Big Bandwidth" is something like the Holy Grail of Net computing: everyone wants instant presence of data, with no hardware or wiring resistance to slow the data down.

BBS. Bulletin Board System. Usually refers to a local user system accessible via modem. Provides proprietary and subscription based services or information. Some BBS servers provide email and other gateways to the **Internet**.

bit. Binary digit. A binary value (that is, a single-digit number in base-2), either 1 or 0. A bit is the smallest unit of digital or computerized data.

Bitnet. The "Because It's Time Network" (originally, "Because It's There"). A global network of computers connected through dedicated telecommunications lines. Operated now as a kind of subnetwork within the **Internet**, but it is rapidly being phased out since it doesn't use Internet **protocols**.

browser. An unfortunately out-of-date term that has stuck to Web **client** programs like Mosaic and Netscape. When most of the information accessible via the Web was text based and graphical, we simply used the viewer software to "browse" requested files. The Web was invented to be a **hypermedia** or multimedia system, so metaphors and terms for software that are based on vision alone are inadequate. A more consistent term for Web interface software is **client** software.

byte. A set of **bits** that represent a single character (like letters, numbers, punctuation). A standard byte is eight bits, though there are bytes formed of larger bit units for some purposes.

CGI. Common Gateway Interface. A method for allowing **HTTP** servers to communicate with a "gateway" on the server for running other interactive programs accessible from a user's Web **client**. The output to a server from fill-in forms, which require a server to process or interpret user input, is the most commonly used CGI application on the Web.

client. Software, like a Web **browser** or **telnet** program, that interacts with, or asks a service from, a **server** on a network. Sometimes you will find the whole system configuration—like your local PC—referred to as a "client system." The Net and Web use client–server architecture, meaning the software and hardware design that makes it work as an interactive system. For example, Netscape, the client software, makes requests of Websites and other **Internet host** systems, the servers, which run the server software.

cracker. A **hacker** who not only breaks into secure computer systems but does so to cause damage or steal information. Crackers generally like to use their computing knowledge and skill against the corporations or power centers that control access to information or hardware. Few hackers cross the line to become crackers.

cross-platform. Software and network systems designed to work on any hardware type or with any **operating system. Internet protocols**, for example, work independently of any specific kind of computer hardware or operating system. Cross-platform design means that incompatible kinds of hardware can be linked by a common way of exchanging or moving **bits**.

cyberspace. The imagined space of graphically represented data in a global computer network. Coined by William Gibson in the novel *Neuromancer* (1984).

cyborg. Cybernetic Organism. Part organic, part inorganic or machine. The cyborg has become a metaphor for a group of ideas pertaining to human–machine interfaces and organic–inorganic combinations as well as for hybrid identities formed in contemporary electronic media culture.

digital. Using the binary method of encoding or representing data. In the digital world, the smallest unit of measure is a **bit**, representing a binary value (1 or 0). Text, images, video, and audio can all be digitized, that is, converted to binary form, and displayed or played on computers. See **analog**.

DNS. Domain Name System. A distributed database system on special **servers** that translate **Internet** computer names (like **whitehouse.gov**) into the numeric addresses actually used by Internet computers (like 198.137.241.30) and vice versa, if needed. In Netspeak we say that names are mapped to numerical addresses, and vice versa. The numeric address is called the "**IP** address." Internet computer names are sorted into domain names, the names you see separated by a dot (".") in an address like **www.loc.gov** (the name for the Library of Congress's Web server). The top-level domains (for example, .edu, .gov, .com, .org, .net or a country abbreviation) are easily recognizable: these are the final abbreviations at the end of an Internet server or host name.

download. Copy or move a file from a **host** system to your local computer.

email. Electronic mail. Messages sent over the **Internet** and **LAN**s from one person to another, or from one person to many. Internet email is edited with a text editor and then sent out as a file through a user's mail **server**.

ethernet. A type of Local Area Network (**LAN**). Computers using **TCP/IP** are frequently connected to the Internet via an ethernet.

FAQ. A net-culture acronym for Frequently Asked Questions. One of the most frequently asked questions about the Net is "What does FAQ mean?" New users, or users new to a body of information on the Net, are advised to read the relevant FAQs before asking questions of other users.

flame. To assault someone else verbally via an email message or messages. Flames can sometimes take the form of angry debates and personal attacks. Flame wars arise when members of a discussion group or list take sides or raise the temperature of a debate. Making prejudicial, personally inflammatory, or unwarranted comments in an email message distributed or posted to a group will usually result in flames from other members of the group.

form. An **HTML** file containing ordinary content and "fields" that can be filled in by users to interact with a Web **server**. The input in a Web form is interpreted by a corresponding program using **CGI** (Common Gateway Interface). Forms can send all kinds of information back to a Web server, which can be processed on the server to do anything—search a database, add a user to a catalog or subscriber list, make a purchase with a credit card, run another program on the server remotely. Web search engines and directories use forms for taking user input, processing the request, and then sending back the requested information.

FTP. File Transfer Protocol; names the **Internet** protocol, program, and process for moving files from one computer to another. Using FTP involves a system **login** on the remote computer, either as an authorized user or as a guest or anonymous user. Like all aspects of user interaction with **Internet** computers, FTP involves a **client** program, which interacts with an FTP **server** that stores and hosts the files. With the FTP client program, a user can **download** files from the FTP server, or if the user has an **account** on the server, **upload** files to a directory on the server.

GIF. Graphical Interchange Format. A digital image format developed by CompuServe to help transfer image files through their online service, but now used universally on the Net, Web, and even CD-ROM applications. A GIF image will have the file extension .gif.

Gopher. A menu-based system for organizing, locating, and distributing files on the **Internet**. Gopher gets its name from its originators at the University of Minnesota (the Golden Gophers), and its obvious utility as a file fetcher, as in it "goes fer" files. As an Internet file delivery system, Gopher uses its own **client–server protocols**. Gopher was the most convenient way to organize and navigate Net files before the Web.

GUI. Graphical User Interface (pronounced "gooey"). The general term for all Windows- and mouse-based user interfaces, such as Macintosh, Microsoft Windows, and **UNIX** X-Windows. Graphical interfaces are distinguished from command line or **shell** interfaces.

hack. *n.* An elegant or creative solution to a computing problem executed by acquired knowledge, experience, or skill rather than by authorized or documented means. *v.* To perform, or attempt to perform, such a computing solution successfully.

hacker. *1.* A person with high-level knowledge of computer systems and networks who enjoys using his or her knowledge and skill for unauthorized use of computer systems. Hackers are usually harmless techies who enjoy the challenge of outsmarting security features on networked computers or using software in creative but unauthorized ways just because it can be done. Some hackers use their skill as a political statement for individual freedom. Compare **cracker**. *2.* A person who enjoys the creative possibilities of programming or modifying programs for its own sake, including unauthorized and undocumented modifications.

hit. *1.* A Net or Web **client** request of a **server** to send a file or perform a computing process. As in "our Web pages get over 100,000 hits per day." *2.* A match between terms (words or phrases) being searched and occurrences of those terms in an electronic database. As in "my search for information on California wines on the Web brought back over 100 hits."

home page. Originally, the term for a Web user's initial file or document, that is, the file that the Web **client** software is configured to load first for the user to navigate Webspace. Now the term most commonly means the starting point or first "page" in a series of linked documents or **hypermedia** files. Each Website, an organized set of information on a Web **server**, has a home page for entry to the world of information presented and organized there.

host. The name for a remote system or **server** on the **Internet**, and usually one that is used to store a large amount of files. The host computer is identified by its domain name and **IP** address. This term is usually synonymous with "server" or "site." The host or server is what the user's local or **client** system accesses. Also used to refer to the computer at the other end of a PC **modem** connection.

hot/hotlink. In Webspeak and multimedia lingo, a section of text or an image is "hot" when a mouse click on a highlighted phrase or section of an image executes a link to another file or location within a file. In a Web **client** program like *Netscape Navigator,* text is usually highlighted to indicate that it contains a hyperlink. An image or graphic can be "image mapped" to execute links to other files or images based on locations (**pixel** coordinates) in the digitized image itself.

HTML. Hypertext Markup Language. The system of tags inserted in Web files that provide formatting instructions and multimedia embedding. HTML is a subset of **SGML**. HTML has gone through several stages, and versions up to HTML 3.0, the current standard now being established. Like all Net and Web standards, HTML is designed as a **cross-platform** standard, independent of any hardware or software.

HTTP. Hypertext Transport Protocol. The **Internet protocol** used by **World Wide Web servers** for transferring files from a Web server to a Web **client**. When you click on a hyperlink that contains a link to another Web file, your client software (like Netscape) makes an HTTP request of the Web server that has the file, and the server responds by sending you the file across the Internet via HTTP.

hypermedia. The method of linking and displaying computer files in more than one **digital** medium (text, audio, image or graphics, and video). Hypermedia expands the **hypertext** concept to embrace all digital media. The Web is a hypermedia system.

hypertext. A kind of document that contains links to other documents. Hypertext documents can be structured in many kinds of relationships, rather than in a restricting hierarchical order or menu. Hypertext is text that is not constrained by physical limits like printed text. On the Web, hypertext links (hyperlinks) allow connections to be made to files and information on many computers around the world. Hypertext is both the conceptual and technical foundation of the Web as a globally distributed system of information.

Internet. The global network of networks connecting thousands of computers via dedicated, high-speed telecommunications lines. The Internet works by allowing many kinds of computers (different hardware types) to communicate through a common **protocol**, **TCP/IP**. Technically speaking, any computer or network of computers that does not transmit and receive data using TCP/IP is not "on the Internet." See **World Wide Web**.

IP. Internet Protocol; see **TCP/IP**. Numerical **Internet** addresses are known as IP addresses.

IRC. Internet Relay Chat; a multi-user program that allows many users to exchange messages simultaneously on the **Internet**. Using IRC requires **client** software and a connection to an IRC **server**.

ISDN. Integrated Services Digital Network. A form of telecommunications link that allows simultaneous voice and data transmission.

ISP. Internet Service Provider. A commercial service that supplies the **Internet** connection for individual users and networks, like an office **LAN** system. For individual users connecting to the Net via a **modem**, the ISP provides the software and hardware link that assigns your computer an IP address and connects your computer to the Net via the ISP's Internet **server** and **router**. Some large ISPs can provide all forms of Internet connectivity, from simple modem dial-up connections via ordinary phone lines to high-speed connections on dedicated data lines.

Java. A **cross-platform** programming language developed by Sun Microsystems and embraced by many Web developers for expanding the capability of Web-deliverable information. Java allows programming to be delivered along with content on the Web, enabling an almost unlimited expansion of the Web's multimedia potential. Java programs, called **applets**, are run by a Web **client** with built-in Java capability or by a helper **application** configured to work with the client.

JPEG/JPG. Joint Photographic Experts Group. A digital image format that uses a standard compression for color images, allowing more graphical information to be stored in smaller files. This image format is used universally on the Web and in some local software and CD-ROM **applications**.

LAN. Local Area Network. A group of computers linked to a central computer (the "LAN server"). All the computers in the network share the software and disk storage available on the network **server**, thus greatly expanding the resources available to a user at any one machine. A LAN has many advantages over standalone PCS: software can be used by everyone on the local net without loading up disk space on individual machines, and files can be stored and saved on a large hard drive and backed up every day for safe storage. LANs can be connected to the **Internet** for worldwide networking, and many people using office computers today get their Internet and **World Wide Web** connection through their LAN.

linkrot. What happens to **hypertext** and **hypermedia** links when people move or remove files on Web **servers** without providing links to new file or server locations. Some files pointed to in URLs just disappear. A feature of bad Website maintenance, but also an inevitability of the globally distributed and dynamic system of the Net and Web.

listserv/listserver. A discussion group in which messages are distributed to an **email** mailing list are generally known as "listserv lists." The computer that runs the listserve software is known as the "listserver." A message posted (sent via email) to a mailing list on a listserver is distributed to all the members or subscribers to the list. Listserv groups are different from **Usenet** newsgroups or **BBS** groups in that messages are sent out to subscribers' personal email addresses rather than simply being posted bulletin-board style for people to read.

login/logout. Connecting to a computer that requires a user ID and a password is called logging in to the system. For example, any computer shared by many users, like a **LAN**, **VAX**, or **UNIX** system, requires a username and a password that allows access to the system. The login gives a user access to an account on a computer system; that is, access to a determined amount of file space on the system's disk and to the programs that run on the system (like an email program and **Internet** utilities like **FTP** and **telnet**). Ending a session on a computer is called logging out, and when a user gives the log out command, the computer ends the connection with the user.

mailing list. General name for various kinds of **email servers** that allow email distribution to members of a list. Email list servers are known by their software types (like **listserv** or listserver, majordomo, and listproc).

MIME. Multipurpose Internet Mail Extensions. A method for allowing the transfer of mixed-media **digital** data (sound, video, image, text) by **Internet email**. The Web uses MIME content-type specifications for transferring a file sent from an **HTTP server** to a **client**. In short, the Web as a multimedia and **hypermedia** system depends on servers and clients knowing the kind of file—the MIME type—being sent and received.

modem. Short for modulater-demodulater. A device used to connect computers via a telephone line or other communications link. When you connect to another computer system via modem (for example, to an **Internet** provider), your modem is making a connection to a modem on the other end via the telephone line. There are now special modems for **ISDN** and cable connections to the Internet.

MOO. MUD, Object Oriented. A form of **MUD** used for educational and social interactive communication. MOO programming languages allow for the creation of virtual environments with various spaces and objects that form a context for MOO virtual identity interaction.

MPEG/MPG. Motion Pictures Expert Group. Defines a compression format for **digital** video and audio used for displaying digital movies.

MUD. Multi-User Dungeon/Multi-User Dimension. Interactive virtual reality role-playing environment on an **Internet server**. Originally invented as a way to play adventure games online, MUD software is now used for many kinds of **real-time** or **synchronous** group interactions. MUD participants assume a virtual identity and interact with other identities according to the rules of the virtual environment defined for that specific MUD.

MUSE. Multi-User Environment. General term for all multi-user **real-time** interactive environments like **MUDs** and **MOOs**.

MUSH. *1.* Multi-User Shared Hallucination. *2.* Multi-User Shell. Another general term for **MUDs** and **MOOs**.

netiquette. Net etiquette. A set of unwritten, commonsense guidelines for appropriate behavior on a shared, worldwide computer network. Learned by interacting with other Net citizens, or "Netizens."

node. A computer on the **Internet**, usually synonymous with server and host. The term is a metaphor for the point where two or more lines of a network intersect.

NNTP. Network News Transport Protocol. The protocol used for transporting **Usenet** articles across the **Internet** to Usenet news **servers**.

Operating System (OS). The basic software that a computer needs to interpret input from a keyboard or mouse, run programs, and read from and write to hard drives and floppy disks. The industry standard for PCs based on Intel microprocessor chips is an operating system developed by Microsoft, hence MS-DOS (Microsoft Disk Operating System) and Microsoft's graphical user interface, Windows. There are several other o-erating systems used today: Macs have their own, **VAX** com-uters run VMS, and **UNIX**. Operating systems also have prog-ms (utilities) for basic system functions like formatting disk-d managing files.

packet. In Netspeak, a bundle of **bits**. O- **Internet**, data files are broken up into smaller chunks -packaged in a kind of envelope that allows the packets t- -onveyed from computer to computer and then reach the- -nation. Depending on the hardware and **digital** mediu- -ket sizes can vary from 40 to 32,000 **bytes**.

pixel. Picture element. T- -lest unit in a **digital** image, appearing as a dot on th- -uter screen. Digital images are measured in pixel size- -ns (for example; a 100 by 200 image is 100 pixels wi- -pixels high). In Web multimedia, each pixel in an image can be defined as a **hypermedia anchor** (a technique known as image mapping), providing a link to another image, file, or document on the Web.

platform. A computer hardware and **operating system** configuration. Examples include the Intel-based PC (running DOS, Windows, and other operating systems), Mac, IBM mainframes, **VAX**, and various systems running **UNIX**. UNIX, however, is a **cross-platform** operating system, written for many kinds of computer hardware.

POP. *1.* Post Office Protocol. The **protocol** used for **Internet email** delivery on an Internet **server**. *2.* Point of Presence. A local access point for an Internet or other communications provider.

port. *1.* Logical: a software-constructed location on a server for listening or opening to different kinds of **protocols** used on a network. **HTTP servers**, for example, use port 80; **telnet** 23; and **Gopher**, 70 by default. But other port numbers can be assigned for special **applications**. You may see a port number after the server name in a URL (for example, **http://home.netscape.com:8080/**). *2.* Physical: a hardware connection for computer input and output. The physical connection for a printer or **modem** on a computer is known as a communications port.

PPP. Point-to-Point Protocol. A method for allowing computers to use **Internet protocols** via a **modem** and telephone line. PPP allows a computer to be assigned an Internet (**IP**) address, and then interact with the Net and Web via **client** software (like Netscape or a **telnet** program). Similar to **SLIP**.

protocol. Instructions or rules that allow two machines to exchange data. The **Internet** is based on a common set of protocols for transferring **digital** information (see **TCP/IP**). Internet protocols are used for transmitting and exchanging data across many miles of connections, allowing any kind of computer to talk to any other.

QuickTim[illegible] The **digital** video format developed by Apple Computer and w[illegible]ely used on the Net and Web. QuickTime files normally have th[illegible]extension .qt.

RAM. Random [illegible]ess Memory. The memory in the computer that can be used by [illegible]grams. When you run a program like your word processing pr[illegible]m or your Web **client**, the programming instructions are tran[illegible]ed from the storage area of disk files to an active area in the [illegible]ter's memory chips. Computer information can be written [illegible]written in the active memory in your computer as the pro[illegible]requires (hence Random Access Memory). The information [illegible] is cleared or removed when you exit a program or turn o[illegible]wer on the computer.

real-time. The transmission of [illegible]he real-world present according to our experience of time [illegible]e communications are usually **synchronous**, like telephone conversations, video conferencing, **MUDs**, and live satellite broadcasts. The **Internet** can be used for real-time communications and information delivery, and there are already successful implementations of real-time video and audio on the Net.

robot. An autonomous program set to perform a task over a network, like indexing file contents on servers or checking **hypertext** links in Web files. See **spider**.

ROM. Read-Only Memory. Information (usually permanent) stored in chips or other media that can only be read by a computer, not written to or changed. All computers have ROM chips that contain basic instructions activated each time you turn the computer on. CD-ROMs used in computing have information stored on them that can be read by the computer (much like an ordinary disk) but not changed, erased, or written to (unlike an ordinary disk).

router. The dedicated computer on a network that reads the addresses on **Internet packets** and routes them to their destination. Any Internet packet may be passed along by several network routers before reaching its final destination.

search engine. A program for searching the contents of files in an indexed database. The Web now has many search engine sites. Web search engines retrieve keyword and phrase matches to contents indexed by Web **spider** or **robot** programs.

server. 1. The computer on any kind of network that stores and delivers files to users' individual workstation computers. 2. On the **Internet**, the term "server" has two senses: the computers, also known as **nodes** or **hosts**, that store and deliver files to other computers on the Net, and the software, like Web server software, that enables the computer to interact with users' computers. As a key component of the **client**–server architecture of the Net, server software interacts with **client** software on individual users' computers.

SGML. Standard Generalized Markup Language. An international standard for writing tags in machine-readable texts files. SGML provides a way to describe the structure and contents of a document in a way that any computer can use. The tags are not displayed but tell software how to interpret and display a document. **HTML** is a reduced subset of SGML.

shell. A **UNIX** term for the "outer" user-access level (command line) to the inner functions (the "kernel") of the **operating system**. Now used to apply to almost any command line interface with a program. A **modem** dial-in **account** in text-only mode on a UNIX **Internet server** is referred to as a "shell account" because commands (for email or Internet file transfers, for example) are typed in on a command line at a system prompt, the user's "shell" for access to the computer. The MS-DOS command line at the "C:\>" or other prompt is also known as the DOS shell.

SLIP. Serial Line Internet Protocol. A method for allowing computers to use **Internet protocols** via a **modem** and telephone line. SLIP allows a computer to be assigned an Internet (**IP**) address, and then interact with the Net and Web via **client** software. Similar to **PPP**.

SMTP. Simple Mail Transfer Protocol. The standard protocol for delivering **email** messages over the **Internet**.

spam. The act of sending out large quantities of unwanted **email** messages to **Usenet** Newsgroups or **Listserv** discussion lists. Net junk mail. This serious breach in **netiquette** will result in **flames**. The term is derived from a Monty Python skit on Spam in which the word "spam" is repeated at comical lengths in restaurant menu items. Relation to actual Spam is uncertain, though association with a canned, processed meat product requires little explanation.

spider. A type of **robot** program that autonomously travels the Web from **server** to server and indexes the contents of publicly accessible files found on the servers. Also called Web walkers, crawlers, and worms. Used by **search engines** for creating searchable indices of Net and Web files.

synchronous. At the same time. Telephone conversations, **Internet Talk**, **IRC**, and **MUD**s are forms of synchronous communications, in which communications are undertaken with the assumption of unnoticeable time intervals between exchanges. Today, many phone communications are **asynchronous**, since we use voice mail and answering machines that allow intervals between communication exchanges.

T-1. A type of telecommunications data line that can transfer data at 1.5 megabits per second (approximately 1.5 million **bits** per second, abbreviated as 1.5 Mbps). Commonly used data line for linking a **LAN** or smaller network to the **Internet**.

T-3. A type of telecommunications data line that can transfer data at 44.7 megabits per second (approximately 44.7 million **bits** per second, abbreviated as 44.7 Mbps). Usually a fiber-optic line. Used to connect larger networks (like regional networks) or heavy-traffic access points (like an **ISP** with many customers and users) to the **Internet**.

Talk/Internet Talk. A program for allowing **synchronous**, **real-time** communication (typed on screen) between two people on **Internet** computers. Requires a Talk **client** program and a connection to **server** software on the other user's computer.

TCP/IP. Transmission Control Protocol/Internet Protocol. The basic set of standard **protocols** that allow data to be transmitted, and transmitted successfully, between computers on the **Internet**. Often simply called **IP**.

telnet. The **Internet** standard **protocol** for connecting two computers on the Net through a remote user **login**. A telnet connection from your local computer (your own PC or workstation) to a remote system on the Net assumes you can log on to that computer with either a secure username and password or a public access login that can be used by anyone. Many library and public information systems allow public access logins for a selected part of the computer system (like a library catalog or public database). After connecting to a remote system (also known as the **host** system or **server**) via telnet, your own local computer becomes a terminal for the remote computer. Like all user-interaction with Internet computers, telnet requires a **client** program running on a user's local computer which establishes the connection to the server.

TIFF. Tag Image File Format, a graphics or image file format developed by Aldus Corporation. TIFF is a standard image format for many graphics programs, and TIFF files can be delivered on the **Internet**. TIFF files have the file extension .tif or tiff.

UNIX. An operating system originally developed by Bell Labs in the 1960s and now existing in many versions for many types of computer hardware. UNIX is a multi-user **operating system** that allows several users to share a computer system simultaneously. Much of the **Internet** runs on UNIX-based computers, and knowing some UNIX concepts and commands can help in understanding how the Internet works. There are versions of UNIX for almost every hardware platform (Intel-based PCS and computers made by Sun Microsystems, DEC, Hewlett-Packard, and IBM), thus making UNIX a kind of universal operating system.

upload. Copy or move a file from your local computer to a **host** system.

URL. Uniform Resource Locator. This is the unique Web address of a file on an **Internet** computer. The URL consists of a resource or **protocol** type (such as **http://**—the Hypertext Transport Protocol specific to the Web), the **host** name or **server** name on the Net, and a file name. For example, **http://home.netscape.com/index.html** is the URL for the **home page** of Netscape Communications Corporation.

Usenet. The large set of newsgroups, also known as discussion groups, on the **Internet**. Usenet Newsgroups operate like global bulletin boards where messages are posted for anyone to read and comment on. Usenet is also a body of rules for establishing and maintaining newsgroups and for using **NNTP**. Usenet groups differ from **listserv** discussion groups in that messages are posted to a common bulletin board rather than being automatically distributed to members' email addresses. See **BBS**.

VAX. The trade name of a minicomputer made by Digital Equipment Corporation (DEC).

Veronica. Very Easy Rodent-Oriented Netwide Index to Computerized Archives. An indexing and searching system for **Gopher** files. Veronica followed **Archie** in the development of **Internet** archiving and indexing tools. Rapidly being superseded by Web indexing and searching software.

virus. A self-replicating computer program that incorporates itself with other software on a computer system. Many viruses are designed to cause harm to the computer **operating system** or to system and data files stored on computer disks. Can be spread from disk to disk or over a network. It is highly unlikely, however, for virus programs to be spread through ordinary Net and Web activity like **email** or server file transfers. All computer users should use, and frequently update, virus scanning and removal software.

VR. Virtual Reality. The reality created by human interaction with computer or **digital** representations and media.

VRML. Virtual Reality Modeling Language. A markup language developed for creating three- dimensional programs and objects that can be delivered over the Web. VRML allows for 3D navigation of objects and content that can be linked to other types of files and content.

VT-100. A computer terminal (monitor and keyboard) invented by Digital Equipment Corporation in the 1970s. This terminal set a standard for text-only interface with computers, and many programs used on the Net are designed for VT-100 terminal emulation, that is, designed to work as if your computer were a VT-100 and could display **ASCII** characters and send commends like a VT-100. If you see this terminal type referred to, it usually means plain-text mode.

WAIS. Wide Area Information Servers. A system and **protocol** for databases on the **Internet**. Largely superseded by the Web and Web file indexing.

wav. An audio file format developed for the Microsoft Windows platform. Files have the .wav file extension.

World Wide Web. A system for delivering and displaying **hypertext** and multimedia files on the **Internet**. The Web uses its own **protocol** on the Net, **HTTP** for transferring files from a Web server to a local user's computer, and Web **client** programs. Since the Web concept includes backward compatibility with earlier Internet protocols like **FTP** and **Gopher**, any Web client program now provides the easiest and most advanced way to use the whole Internet. With the Web interface provided by the client program, retrieving information on the Net is done via hypertext or **hypermedia** links, rather than by making choices on hierarchical menus or by typing commands at a system prompt. The Web enables users to access information in all kinds of formats and file types (text, image, graphics, sound, and video) through one user interface or front end.

zine. An alternative magazine, sometimes in electronic format. Most zines have small circulations and are published for a specific reading community like those interested in experimental art forms and music. A whole subculture of fan zines has grown up in the past two decades. There are now many Webzines, multimedia zines published only on the Web.

Bibliography

The philosophy of *Web Works* has been that the Web contains the most up-to-date information about the Net and Web. But here are some suggestions for further reading, if you want to go beyond the information in this book or explore other ideas.

General Guides to the Net and Web

December, John, and Neil Randall. *The World Wide Web Unleashed.* 3rd ed. Indianapolis: Sams.Net Publishing, 1996.

Gilster, Paul. *The New Internet Navigator.* New York: John Wiley, 1995.

Krol, Ed. *The Whole Internet.* 2nd ed. Sebastopol, Calif.: O'Reilly, 1994.

Stout, Rick. *The World Wide Web Complete Reference.* Berkeley, Calif.: Osborne McGraw-Hill, 1996.

Guides to HTML

Graham, Ian S. *HTML Source Book.* 2nd ed. New York: John Wiley, 1996.

Lemay, Laura. *Teach Yourself Web Publishing with HTML in a Week.* Indianapolis: Sams.Net Publishing, 1995.

Unix Guides

Hahn, Harley. *Unix Unbound.* Berkeley, Calif.: Osborne McGraw-Hill, 1994.

Levine, John, and Margaret Levine Young. *Unix for Dummies.* Foster City, Calif.: Foster City, Calif.: IDG, 1993.

Norton, Peter and Harley Hahn. *Peter Norton's Guide to Unix.* New York: Bantam Computer, 1991.

Net, Web, Hypertext, Cybertheory, and Digital Culture

Cotton, Bob, and Richard Oliver. *The Cyberspace Lexicon: An Illustrated Dictionary of Terms from Multimedia to Virtual Reality.* London: Phaidon, 1994.

Landow, George P. *Hypertext: The Convergence of Contemporary Critical Theory and Technology.* Baltimore: Johns Hopkins University Press, 1992.

Landow, George P., ed. *Hyper/Text/Theory*. Balitimore: Johns Hopkins University Press, 1994.
Lanham, Richard. *The Electronic Word: Democracy, Technology, and the Arts*. Chicago: University of Chicago Press, 1993.
Mandel, Thomas, and Gerard Van der Leun. *Rules of the Net: Online Operating Instructions for Human Beings*. New York: Hyperion, 1996.
Mitchel, William J. *City of Bits: Space, Place, and the Infobahn*. Cambridge, Mass.: MIT Press, 1995.
Negroponte, Nicholas. *Being Digital*. New York: Knopf, 1995.
Rheingold, Howard. *The Virtual Community: Homesteading on the Electronic Frontier*. New York: HarperCollins, 1994.
Taylor, Mark, and Esa Saarinen. *Imagologies: Media Philosophy*. New York: Routledge, 1994.

A Brief Guide to *Netscape Navigator* Features

Note: Online help for using *Netscape Navigator* is always available by clicking on the **Handbook** button in the Directory Button row or by clicking on **Help | Handbook** in the top menu bar.

The *Netscape Navigator* Screen

Pull-Down Menus Click for menus of commands.

Toolbar Buttons Click for basic navigation features.

Location Line Displays URL for current file. Label changes to "Go To" when you delete current URL.

Directory Buttons Shortcuts to information on the Netscape Website.

Main Window Where the files from Internet servers are displayed. (You have the option of hiding the Toolbar, the Location line, and the Directory Buttons to open more display area in the main window. Click on **Options** to remove or add the display of navigation tools.)

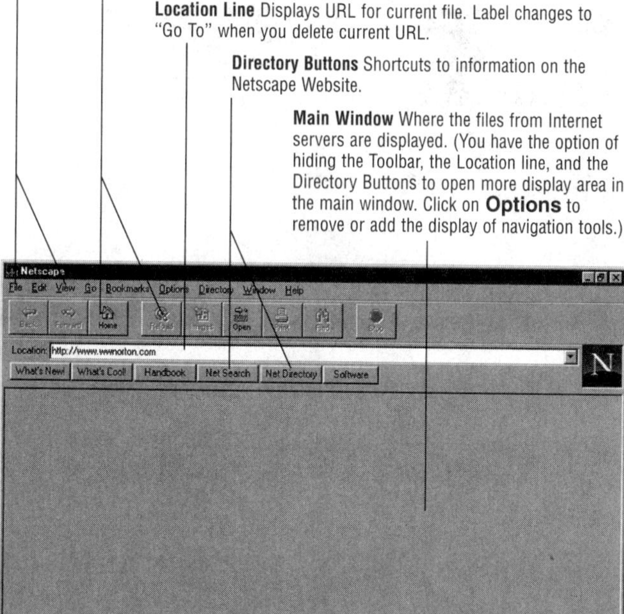

Mail icon Click to open email window to do email within Netscape. (You must first be properly configured for your mail server in the **Options** | **Mail** and **News Preferences** | **Servers** screen.) A question mark appears if Netscape cannot automatically check email messages.

Status Line Displays the URL in the hotlink that the mouse currently points to. Useful to see where a hotlink takes you before you click on it. Changes to download status information when a file is loading.

Key Secure (encrypted) or nonsecure (nonencrypted) server symbol. (Broken key means you are interacting with an open access server with no encrypted or protected data; unbroken key means you are using a secure server with encrypted data.)

Quick-Start Guide to Basic Navigation: Using the Toolbar and Directory Buttons

The Toolbar and Directory Buttons provide quick navigation. They overlap with the full features and commands in the pull-down menu items.

Toolbar Buttons

Back Go to the previously viewed page. Reloads the last visited page in the history list of files that Netscape has loaded. (The "history list" is a record of the visited pages in your current Netscape session.)

Forward Go to the next page in the history list.

Home Loads the home page (starting page) currently configured. (Change your default home page by using the **Options** | **General Preferences** screen. Enter a URL of your choice in the "Start With" dialog box.)

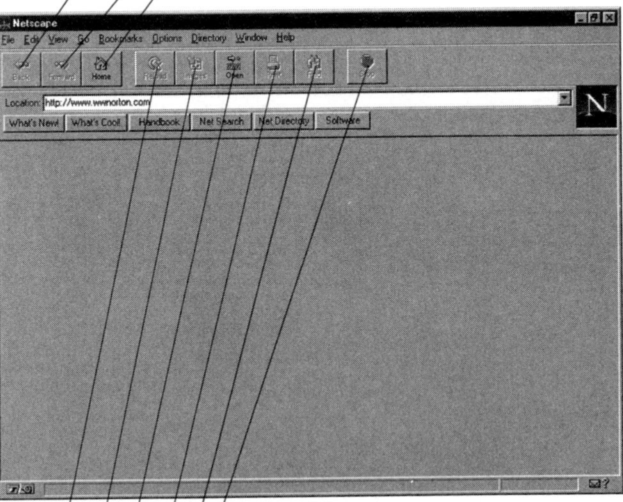

Stop Stops the current file transfer from a server. Useful if the transfer stalls or if you want to make a different choice. You can Reload after you stop a transfer.

Find Allows a keyword search of the file currently displayed. Type in a keyword in the dialog box that appears.

Print Prints the document in the main Netscape window.

Open Allows you to enter a new URL. This button duplicates the Location line functions.

Images If you have turned the display of inline images off (using the **Options** | **Autoload** images feature), this button restores the display of images.

Reload Reloads the current page. Netscape sends out a new request to the server to send the file. Important for pages that change. (Note: Netscape can reload visited pages from its cache memory, but a cached file will be the version previously viewed, not an updated one directly from the server.)

Directory Buttons

Directory buttons are quick links to pages maintained by Netscape Communications Corporation for Web users.

What's New! Goes to a page of recent and interesting new Websites. Updated frequently; visit often.

What's Cool! The name says it all. The Web has been cool from the beginning, and this page will keep you up-to-date on the newest and most creative Websites around the world.

Handbook The online handbook for using *Netscape Navigator.* A full overview of all software features.

Net Search Quick link to Web search engines. Netscape's search engine page is constantly updated to include new search sites and indices.

Software Link to pages of information about Netscape software, including how to download new versions of *Netscape Navigator.*

Net Directory Quick link to a group of starting points for Web navigation.

Menu Items

Netscape Navigator's pull-down menus offer access to all the features of the software. The features are too extensive to describe here; they can be learned by going to the Menu page in the online Handbook (click on the Handbook Directory Button or **Help | Handbook**) and by simple experimentation.

Here are some features in the menus that you will want to learn after you have used the basic navigation tools in the Toolbar and Directory Buttons. (Advanced features and those duplicated in the Toolbar and Directory Buttons are omitted.)

File
| **Open File** Load a file from a local disk drive (usually a: or c:).
| **Save As** Save the currently displayed file (and rename it, if you wish) to a local disk drive.
| **Exit/Quit** Exit or quit Netscape.

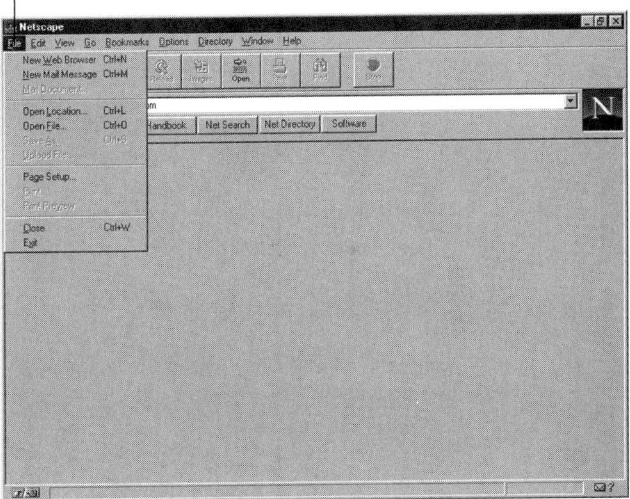

Edit

| **Copy** Copy the highlighted area to the Windows clipboard. Highlight text to be copied by dragging the mouse over the selected area first.

| **Paste** Paste clipboard contents. Useful for inserting text into Location line.

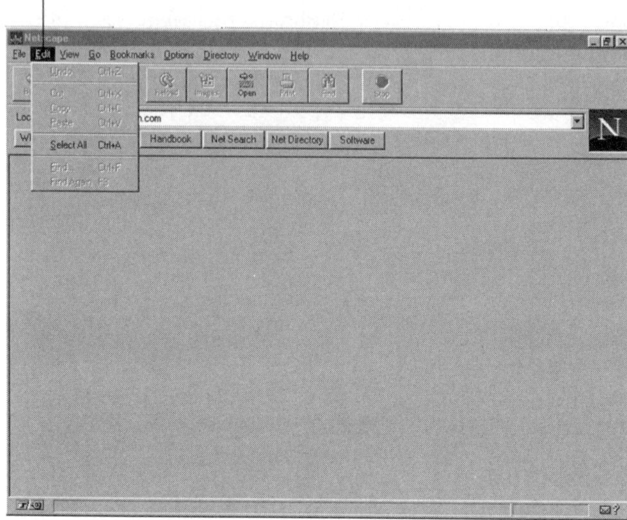

View

| **Document Source** Displays the source HTML file in a separate window. Useful for studying the HTML markup and design of a Web page. Text in source file can be copied into your own HTML files.

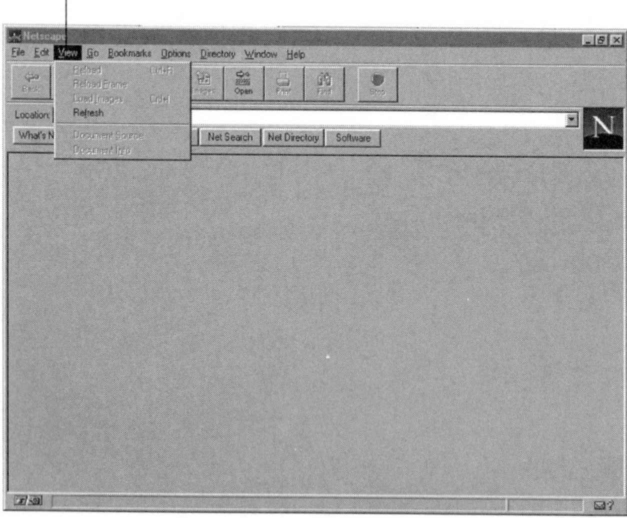

Go
History list (recently viewed pages) appears at bottom of this menu. Useful for jumping to a previously viewed page.

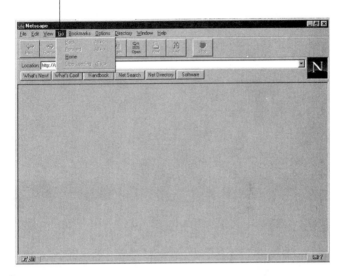

Bookmarks
| **Add bookmark** Add the URL of the currently displayed page to your Bookmarks list. Bookmarks will display at bottom of menu.
| **Go to Bookmarks** Edit and organize your Bookmarks list.

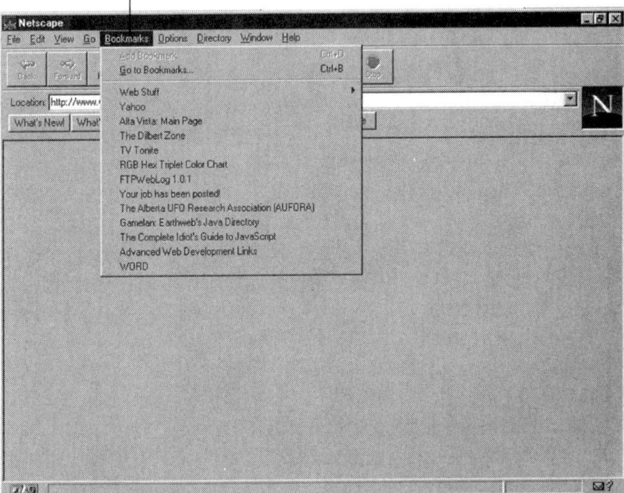

Options

| **General Preferences** Customize Netscape, configure helper applications, and set up network connections for email and Usenet Newsreader.

| **Show . . .** Hide navigation tools to open up more display area. Click on Show Toolbar, Location, or Directory Buttons to turn on or off the display of these items in your Netscape window.

| **Auto Load Images** Click to turn off display of inline images. Useful for faster loading of files if you want only the basic text information.

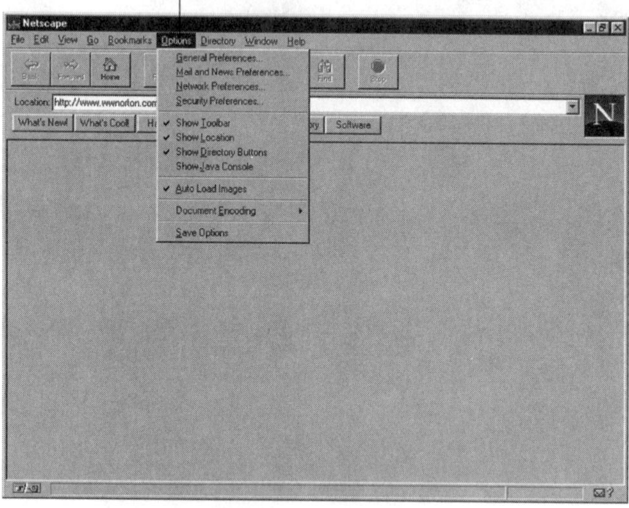

Directory

Duplicates Directory Buttons. Use if you have turned them off under Options.

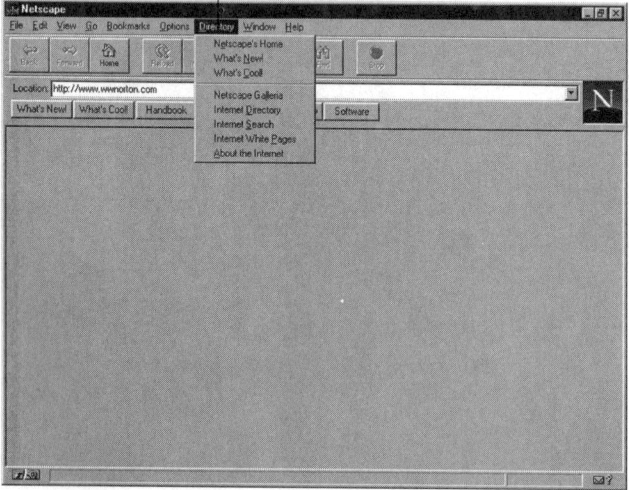

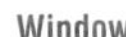

Window
Opens Netscape email and Newsreader windows.

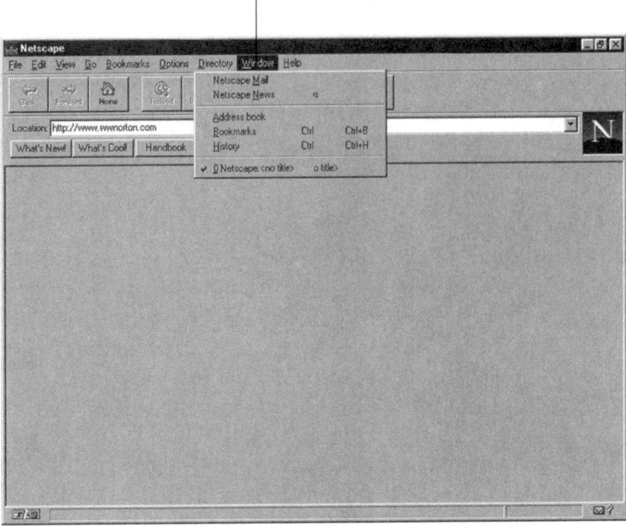

Help
Basic help files and Netscape information.

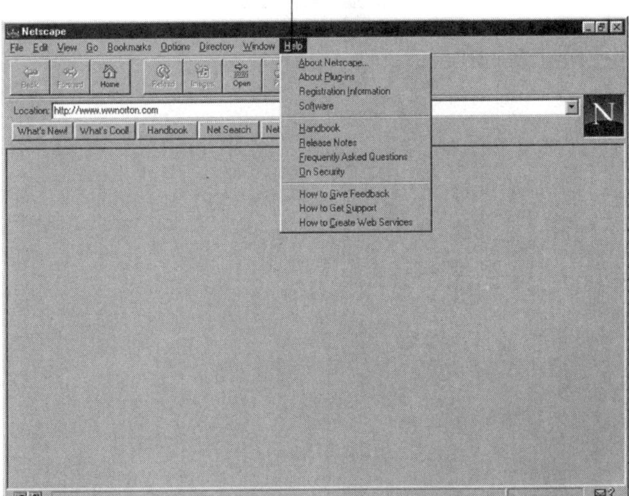

Netscape Shortcuts

- Go to a new URL quickly by typing it in the Location line. Click on the Location line to highlight the current URL. Type in the new URL that you want to go to. The old URL will automatically be deleted as you begin typing. (You can also delete the current URL and type in a new one in a black Location line.) Then hit Enter, and Netscape will fetch and display the new file. Further tip: you can paste text into the Location line also; if you find a reference to a URL cited in some other file, simply copy it and paste it into the Location line. Then hit Enter.
- URL shortcut: To save time when typing in new URLs, omit the "http://" in Web URLs. Netscape defaults to the "http" resource type (the Web protocol) when reading new URLs typed on the Location line. For example, to go to the Library of Congress Website, just type in "www.loc.gov" in the Location line and hit the Enter key. Netscape will supply the Web protocol, and the URL will display as "http://www.loc.gov" on the Location line.
- The quickest URL shortcut: Netscape defaults to both the commercial ("com") Internet domain and the "www." convention for naming Web servers. For example, to go to IBM's Website, simply type in "ibm" and hit Enter. Netscape will supply the resource type (the "http" protocol), the "www." server designation, and "com" at the end of the server name. The URL will then display as "http://www.ibm.com".

Index

Notes

Notes

Notes